PENANG
IN 12 DISHES

HOW TO EAT LIKE YOU LIVE THERE

redporkpress

ARCHITECTURE
IN UNESCO-LISTED
GEORGE TOWN

CONTENTS

THE VIEW FROM
THE GOLDEN
SANDS RESORT

ABOUT PENANG

PENANG is **charming and laid-back**, with a multi-cultural mix of inhabitants; its mosques, churches and temples, both Chinese and Tamil, speak to this. Streets in the **historic core of George Town**, its lovely little capital, are **UNESCO heritage-listed**. Up the coast are gorgeous swathes of resort-dotted beaches, the interior steams with **pockets of lush jungle**, and clusters of condominiums dazzle in the sun. With a burgeoning high-tech industry, it's go-ahead. Old and new, east and west, resolutely traditional but never insular and, while a touch conservative, not uptight; **Penang has so much to offer**.

The Brits claimed Penang in 1786 but it was **an important trading port** before that. A strategic position on the Straits of Malacca had lured merchants – from India, the Middle East and China – for centuries. Ultimately **the British came**; it was Francis Light who convinced the then Sultan of Kedah to hand over Penang to the British East India Company. During the 19th century, **trade in spices, betel nut, tin, opium and rice** made Penang wealthy; its importance declined somewhat with the rise of Singapore and the loss of its tax-free port status in the 1960s.

Although it's the island that lures visitors, Penang Island is part of a larger Malaysian province that takes in a bit of the mainland, 8km away. It's **the smallest province in Malaysia** and, with a population of around 1.7 million, has Malaysia's highest population density. George Town is Malaysia's second most populous city. The island is irregularly shaped, with a hilly interior giving way to narrow coastal plains. In the southwest corner are the island's **last remaining pockets of farmland and orchards**; it's scenic here and dotted with rustic fishing villages.

Bahasa is the official language, but Hokkien, Tamil, English and Mandarin are widely spoken. **Street names are the original English ones** so getting around is simple. There are, in effect, two Penangs; the first is found in the **louche, seaside vibes of Batu Ferringhi**, with its beachfront hotels, foot spas and restaurants. There's not much to do **except lie in the sun**, splash in a pool or chuck a frisbee. Water ▷

sports such as parasailing and jet-skiing are popular, and many folk are content to stay put here. Then there's heritage Penang, centring on George Town, with **quaint streets and that vibrant, cultural mix.** This is one of the **best preserved pre-war enclaves in South-East Asia** and its old architecture is an amazing coalescence of English, Chinese, Indian and Islamic elements. For the purposes of this book, we've pretty much concentrated on George Town and around, with a few forays up the beautiful coast for good, balanced measure.

Penang has a **year-round equatorial climate**, with average highs ranging from 28C-32C. March is generally the hottest month and there are two wet seasons. The first is April to May and the second, from September to October. **High season for tourism here is December through January** and low season, during September and October.

Some festivals in Penang

Hari Raya Aidilfitri: the end of the fasting month, Ramadan. A three-day celebration of feasting, this is a very big holiday, even for non-Muslims.

Chinese New Year: celebrated over 15 days and ending on the 15th night of the first lunar moon of the year. Houses are cleaned, new clothes are worn, feasts are eaten, lanterns are lit and gifts exchanged.

Thaipusam: a Hindu festival, celebrated January/February, marking the victory of good over evil. It begins with a procession along Lebuh Queen to the Nattukottai Temple.

Wesak Day: Buddha's birthday. Adherents cleanse themselves, seek blessings and finish off with a colourful procession through the city. Celebrated on the 15th day of the 4th lunar month.

Hungry Ghost Festival: in the 7th lunar month. The Chinese community stage puppet and other street performances for the dead, make offerings at temporary altars erected around town, and burn paper money.

Mid-Autumn Festival: falling on the 15th day of the 8th lunar month, this Chinese festival is marked by the giving of moon cakes.

Merdeka: August 31, Malaysian Independence Day. Unbridled patriotism – flags flying, an early morning parade and cultural shows.

Deepavali: a Tamil Hindu festival falling sometime in October or November. Also called The Festival of Lights, it's when people share food, light lamps in homes and businesses and set off fireworks.

大成印務公司

404

TAI SENG PRINTING CO..

成印務 有限公司

op Tai Seng Printing Sdn. Bhd.

大成務公司

A STREET IN
GEORGE TOWN

ABOUT PENANG FOOD

'Prince of Wales Island'. 'The Pearl of the Orient'. 'The First Island'. 'The Silicon Valley of The East'. 'The Island of the Area Nut Palm'. Penang has worn many titles (the latter is a literal translation of its Malay name, Pulau Pinang), but for the culinary traveller, only one moniker matters: **'Gastronomic Freaking Nirvana'**. Few places on earth boast such a concentration of delicious, authentic and affordable fare as does Penang. It's one of the great bastions of street food in Asia, if not the world.

Because of the **Indian, Chinese and Malay** threads running through the cuisine, the local repertoire is **diverse and extensive**. From Indian curries, breakfast and tiffin fare (*appam, idli* and *thosai*, for example) and tandoori, to soothing Chinese congee, dim sum, noodle dishes and cakes to spicy Malay stir fries, soup noodles, salads and icy sweets to finessed Nyonya specialities to seafood ... the choice can be a little overwhelming.

Penang is, arguably, **most famous for its hawker dishes**. You're not likely to find yourself in restaurants so much as at hawker centres and in casual old *kopi tiams* (coffee shops). With their **delightfully retro interiors,** hawker carts set up outside or, more permanently, just inside. These produce their specialities for passers-by as well as for coffee shop customers. You order food from the hawkers and pay them, then order drinks from the *kopi tiam* staff, and pay them separately.

Hawker food is incredibly affordable and locals take many of their meals out. Why would you cook at home, when food is so cheap (and so good) on the street? Breakfast usually consists of *roti canai* (see pg 14), with curried gravy or *dhal*. Or an order of toast with half-cooked eggs and *kaya*, a jam made using coconut, egg and *pandan* leaf. *Char koay teow, char koay th'ng, chee cheong fun* or some other noodle dish, ▷

Nasi Lemak

Kapitan Keling Mosque

Curry puffs

Dim sum

Toh Soon Cafe

Cheong Fatt Tze Mansion

Street art in George Town is famous

CHICKEN RICE
FROM A GEORGE
TOWN HAWKER

nasi lemak, rice porridge (*congee*) or dim sum are also popular in the morning. For lunch and dinner, the choices broaden further: barbecued meats, *Hokkien mee*, *laksa*, *rojak*, *mee goreng*, *nasi kandar*, banana leaf rice, *biryani* and seafood. In between, there are **endless snacking possibilities** – sweet biscuits and iced desserts, traditional rice flour-based cakes, sticks of *satay* or luscious, fresh, tropical fruits.

Eating here is a practical exercise in anthropology and history, as the **food reflects all the migration, assimilation and intermarriage** that have made Penang what it is today. In some dishes, you'll notice the complex piquancy of **Malay cooking** meeting **Chinese ingredients** and techniques. Indian spices flavour cherished curries, *dhals* and gravies. Chilli-hot, fresh-herbal, lime-infused notes hint at Penang's **proximity to Thailand**. Pungent *belacan* (fermented shrimp paste), whiffy *heh ko* (prawn paste), caramelly *gula melaka* and puckery tamarind are unmistakably local flavours, and also ones that overlap a little with neighbouring Indonesia. Halal Mamak and Malay dishes speak of Islamic influence. Toasted bread with butter for breakfast has **English colonisation** written all over it. Plenty of dishes attest to the predominance of Chinese in the population in Penang – the highest of any Malaysian region. The melting pot nature of Penang's cuisine makes it both wholly unique and utterly compelling.

Many hawker cooks are second or third generation, and make their dishes according to **family recipes, unchanged for decades**. It's this constancy that has preserved Penang's food ways so well; this and the discerning, **food-savvy locals** who know where the ultimate examples of any particular dish are found – and who is off the boil. As a visitor, it's best not to get caught up in the 'best of' mentality when it comes to a dish, as this can literally do your head in. It's unlikely you'll have terrible food, no matter where you eat. Portions of hawker food aren't large, making it **perfect for a grazing approach**. And it's so affordable that, on the off chance you do order a dud, it won't break any banks.

Eateries, and **hawker cooks, keep varying hours** – they're certainly not uniform across Penang. Partly this depends on the style of food; some *kopi tiams* close in the afternoon – others stay open all day. Some carts appear in the late afternoon or evening – others just ply the morning trade. ▷

Still other places (notably some of the large restaurants in Little India) are open 24/7, but will run a different menu in the morning from the evening. Places shut on different days of the week too and some close on the same day, but on alternating weeks. Sole traders can decide not to open on a certain day for whatever reason, or shut up early, or open late. So, while the business hours given in this book were accurate at the time of writing, on Penang Island, things can change fast. ✤

The iconic dish, *char koay teow*

Fresh lychees

A *kopi tiam* sign

Outside Lone Pine hotel

Indian sweets

ROTI TELUR AND
CHICKEN CURRY AT
JALAN TRANSFER

Twirl about, slap around, stretch thin, fold over, roll out, repeat. Then fry up, flip a bit and smash with bare hands to break the whole thing up; the skills required to make light, flaky *roti canai* are more akin to conjuring than cooking.

ROTI CANAI

Roti canai (pronounced 'chanai') is made by Mamaks, or Indian Muslim cooks, mostly at carts and stalls. Or at least in very informal restaurant scenarios. It's similar to a Southern Indian flat bread called *paratha*, which originated with Sri Lankan Tamils. *Roti* means 'bread' in Malay; the *'canai'* part might be a reference to Chennai (Madras), from where many immigrant workers came. Or, it could literally be the Malaysian word *'canai'*, which means 'to roll out dough'. Served with a side of *dhal* (spiced lentils) or any number of other curries (chicken and vegetable are common), it's the breakfast of choice across all of Penang's ethnicities. And it's not hard to see why. *Roti canai* is seriously delicious; a slightly oily, wheat flour-based flat bread constructed around fine layers, with a crispish exterior and unbelievably soft, chewy innards. ▷

ROTI CANAI

In English and Hokkien, *roti canai* is sometimes called 'flying' bread in reference to the way it's made. Indeed, the fine sheets of dough do almost seem to sail though the air as each is stretched, turned and folded multiple times. The point of this is to create maximum layers and incorporate as much air into the layers as possible; this is what makes the cooked bread light and puffy.

Egg-filled *roti* with curry gravy

The shiny and slippery dough is made by kneading together ghee, flour and water. Sometimes a little condensed milk is included as well, and many vendors buy their dough ready made. After repeated bouts of flattening, oiling and folding, individual balls of the dough are left to sit and relax a bit. Next, each ball is stretched and rolled so it's paper thin, then it's gathered into a rope-like shape that's wound into a spiral and flattened. The rounds are fried to order on a hot griddle with a little ghee or margarine. *Roti canai* can be plain or filled (with eggs, onion, sardines or margarine, for example) and, when filled, the rolled-out dough is folded over the filling to seal it in and form a square-shaped bread. Plain *roti* is sometimes called *roti kosong*. *Roti canai banjir* means 'flooded' and it's when *roti* comes pre-torn and smothered in curry. Otherwise, you rip pieces off and dip in a side dish of curry, *dhal* or gravy, as you eat. ❖

Just cooked *roti*

At Jalan Transfer

Various curries for roti

kari ayam:
chicken curry

kari daging:
beef curry

kari kambing:
mutton curry

kari campur:
mixed curry (you choose which curries you want)

kari dhal:
lentil curry

kari kacang kuda:
chickpea curry

dalcha:
vegetable-lentil curry (potatoes, carrot, tomatoes, green chilli and the like)

Chicken curry, Jalan Transfer

17

Roti variations

roti telur: filled with egg

roti tisu: paper thin and particularly flaky

roti bawang: filled with onion

roti telur bawang: filled with egg and onion

roti bom: smaller, thicker *roti* with the dough in a spiral; often served with sugar and margarine

roti planta: filled with margarine and sugar

roti sardin: stuffed with canned sardines and sometimes sambal

roti pisang: filled with banana

roti sayur: stuffed with vegetables such as spinach

roti durian: stuffed, in season, with, well, you can guess what

roti kaya: filled with *kaya* (coconut and egg jam)

STREET *ROTI* VENDOR NEAR PRANGIN MALL, GEORGE TOWN

Penang Street Famous Roti Canai

WHERE TO EAT

SPECIAL FAMOUS ROTI CANAI
56 Jalan Transfer, George Town
6.30am-1pm, 3.30pm-7pm, daily
Strung along the footpath under a series of canopies, this is heralded as Penang's best roti canai place. The roti are fluffy, the curries aromatic, the servers friendly and the atmosphere buzzy. Punters on scooters pull in for takeaway, people jostle for seating and the folding and flipping of roti making is never-ending.

Cooking roti telur

PENANG STREET FAMOUS ROTI CANAI
Cnr Lebuh Bishop and Lebuh Penang, George Town
6.30am-3pm (closed Sunday)
A cheap, old-school hangout that could easily be missed – it's right outside Veloo Villas (see pg 43). They make roti jala (see pg 43) and roti telur bawang as well as roti canai and are known for their fabulous beef curry. The simple menu also has a great chicken curry.

Roti Canai Jalan Argyll

ABU MAMAK
Cnr Jalan Dato Koyah and Jalan Penang, George Town
7.30pm-6.30am, daily
A place for nocturnals as it only opens at night, in what used to be a car park. The roti are particularly flaky. Indulge in a cheese-filled roti bom slathered in condensed milk – there's kaya involved in this version too. Yes, really. If you think that's weird, check out the roti samurai, a whole pile of incongruous stuff (sausage, cheese, mayo, smarties), slathered on a roti.

SRI ANANDA BAHWAN
53 Lebuh Penang, George Town
7am-12am, daily
Choose between six curries and a choice of regular canai or thin roti tisu, and dine in air-conned comfort. One for those anxious about eating on the side of the road; do order their sweet, milky Madras tea.

ROTI CANAI JALAN ARGYLL
Jalan Argyll, George Town
6.30am -12.30pm, daily
Low-key and local in feel (it's a little away from the tourist hoopla), they've been around since 1955 and have carved quite a reputation. Their meat curries are especially meaty so prepare for a protein hit and a half, if you drop by for brekkie. Roti banjir here is a 'flood' of three different curry gravies and they're renowned for it.

Breakfast

Breakfast; there are just so many ways to slice and dice it. *Roti canai. Hokkien mee. Mee goreng. Nasi lemak. Rice porridge.* Yadda yadda yadda.

A SERVE OF
ROTI BENGAL

But if you fancy some local-style toast, eggs and jam, you're sorted too. Oh, and coffee and tea? No worries. Here's where to breakfast, what to order and some essential early morning vocab, for good measure.

Half-cooked eggs: these come as standard with most versions of toast. They are very sloppy and some might say, an acquired taste. They often arrive in a cup and you're meant to liquidise them by stirring in soy sauce and white pepper, then use as a dip for toast.

Kaya: a curd-like jam made from egg, sugar and coconut, flavoured with pandan leaf. Its colour depends on the amount of cooking, degree of sugar caramelisation and quantity of pandan used; Nyonya *kaya* is quite green whereas most versions are brownish. It has a rich, custard-like texture – the word 'kaya' means 'rich' in Malay. Decent places will make their own.

Kopi tiam: literally 'coffee shop'. There are *kopi tiams* all over George Town, mainly family run and with interiors delightfully freeze-dried in time. They're unpretentious and are where locals head for simple meals, including coffee, *kaya* and toast in the mornings. Generally you'll find hawker carts pulled up outside, offering a variety of fare – *char koay teow, chee cheong fun, wan tan mee,* etc. It's fully expected you'll eat the hawker fare in the *kopi tiam,* accompanied by in-house coffee. ▷

Cutting bread at Roti Bakar Hutton Lane

21

BREAKFAST

Roti bakar: 'grilled bread', a.k.a. toast

Roti bengal: toast topped with butter and two half-cooked eggs

Roti kahwin: toasted bread, or soft bun, topped with *kaya* and slabs of butter

Roti balut telur: thick slices of white bread dipped in beaten egg, griddle-cooked, then served cut in small pieces, scattered generously with white sugar

Roti Taiwan: toast with peanut butter, sprinkled with chopped, roasted peanuts

Telur ayam kampong: if you see this on a menu board, it means eggs (*telur*) from a 'village' i.e. free range

Teh terak: literally 'pulled' tea. Hot tea is combined with evaporated or condensed milk and poured between two vessels from a height, resulting in a foamy mixture that cools slightly as it's made. The tea is not high grade and it's believed the aeration improves flavour. Associated with Mamaks, it is often served with *roti canai*.

Coffee: 'white' coffee originated in Ipoh, not far from Penang. Coffee beans are roasted to a light colour with margarine, which gives a strong caramel flavour and results in a gooey mass. Left to harden, it is broken up then ground into a powder. Many manufacturers mix in powdered creamer and sugar. Black coffee, called *kopi-o*, is made by roasting the beans with margarine, sugar and wheat. It's brewed in an open vessel on a stovetop then strained into cups through a stocking-like tube of fabric and enriched with condensed milk. A good *kopi-o* should be thick, strong and sweet. It can be ordered without milk and also as *kopi ice* (literally poured over a glass of ice). ✤

Roti balut telur

Half-cooked eggs and toast

Making *teh terak*

Toh Soon Cafe

WHERE TO EAT

TOH SOON CAFE
**184 Lebuh Campbell,
George Town
8am-6pm (closed
Sunday)**
Popular with a capital 'pop'. Folk edge into the tight laneway set-up even before they've stoked up the charcoal contraption used to toast bread. They're famous for their way of toasting: a guy spends his day crouched over the fire, patiently turning bread until it's crisp and slightly smoky. They bake bread at their own factory and even offer a low-calorie option. Toast with *kaya*, peanut butter or just butter is the way to go.

ROTI BAKAR HUTTON LANE
**300 Jalan Phee Choon,
George Town
4am-1pm, daily**
With its awesome outdoors location (just off Jalan Penang) and friendly, bearded boss man, this is great. Since 1967, they've been making *roti canai* and charcoal-grilled toasts, but it's the yum, egg-soaked *roti balut telur* that will get your pulse racing. It's thick, fluffy, rich and crunchy with sugar.

ENG LOH KOPI TIAM
**48 Lebuh Gereja,
George Town
8am-3pm (closed
Sunday)**
Plastic chairs, chipped

BREAKFAST

veneer table tops, fans lazily swinging around... the decor is pure *kopi tiam* at its finest. The corner position makes for excellent people watching and it's just over the road from the Pinang Peranakan Mansion (see pg 104). Order the *roti* Taiwan, slathered in margarine, peanut butter and nuts. They also do a garlic toast and unique Sarawak '3 Layer' tea.

00 WHITE COFFEE CAFE
**262 Lebuh Carnarvon,
George Town
8am-9.30pm (closed
Wednesday)**
As the name suggests, they make a thing of traditional Ipoh white coffee; you can have it with evaporated milk, condensed milk, a mix of both, with neither or just with sugar. Their toast menu runs the gamut – they even do steamed *kaya* toast, cutely served in a bamboo basket.

ENG AUN KOPI TIAM
**201 Lebuh Kimberley,
George Town
6.30am-12pm (closed
Monday)**
In a corner spot, this is a fabulous place to sit and commune with locals. In operation for 60 years, they make a mean coffee and attract a big line-up of hawker carts – look for the guy selling homemade *kuih* (see pg 127) just outside, in the morning.

23

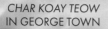

*CHAR KOAY TEOW
IN GEORGE TOWN*

'Stir-fried noodles' sounds too prosaic a name for an iconic dish but that's essentially what this is. Throw in sprouts, a slosh of duck egg, crunchy lardy bits, a scatter of cockles, garlic chives, sweet, toothsome prawns and plenty of *wok hei*, and you've got something else entirely.

CHAR KOAY TEOW

A good *char koay* (also spelled *kway*) *teow* is sublime. Smoky, slippery, smooth, chewy and with oodles of sweet-salty savour, it's an unmissable meal. It comes from the Hokkien tradition (*char* means 'fried' and *koay teow* is the rice noodle part) and, while it's common thoroughout much of South-East Asia, it's those prawns, that *bak eu pok* (fried lard cubes), the cockle flesh and beansprouts that make the Penang version unique. Often there will be slices of *lap cheong* (Chinese pork sausage) as well. The noodles (fresh, unrefrigerated rice noodles; putting them in the fridge makes them hard), are thinner than what you'll find in, say, Singapore or Southern Malaysia, and Penang CKT is less sweet too.

You might get the choice of duck or chicken egg – locals love creamy duck, which is slightly more expensive. Vendors will likely ask "You want spicy?" Which of course, you do. Even so, CKT isn't overly chilli-hot, ▷

COOKING *CHAR KOAY TEOW*, ONE PORTION AT A TIME

Pieces of deep-fried lard

Fresh rice noodles

Sisters Char Koay Teow

炒粿條炒麵
CHAR KOAY TEOW & MEE
蛋 E99 小 RM5·00   Without E99 RM4·30

27

CHAR KOAY TEOW

with just a little chilli paste and some soy sauce added during cooking. Essential to a good CKT is an exceptionally hot, well-seasoned wok to produce the elusive *wok hei* or 'breath of the wok', that gives the dish its delicious, subtle smokiness and caramelly taste; without this, it's not a good rendition. It takes skill to impart proper *wok hei* and get the sweet/spicy/salty/smoky balance perfect.

Cooks will generally make one portion of CKT at a time, over an industrial-strength gas supply or charcoal burner. This is to maintain the highest possible heat and, during busy periods, it's not unusual to wait 20 minutes or so for your serve to be cooked. Generating the required heat is not something that can be easily achieved at home so people go out for their CKT. It's thought the dish started as a simple, calorie-rich noodle dish to sustain workers and it evolved from there. Most modern versions have cut back on lard and oil in line with growing health consciousness, although really, a portion of CKT isn't huge. It was once standard to serve it on a banana leaf (you'll still see this at a few places), to enhance the flavour.

Waiting at Hock Ban Hin coffee shop

CKT is ubiquitous and fierce debate rages constantly about whose is best. One vendor will be the bees knees one month, and spurned the next. "Too arrogant" and "too expensive" are the regular complaints when an outlet falls from grace. Experts know who cooks with lard, whose blend of soy sauce is just right, who's skimping on the freshest prawns and who is still wokking over charcoal. It's a quick meal eaten throughout the day, but some cooks only fire up in the evening; others concentrate on the morning and lunch trade. ✤

Delivering plates of CKT

WHERE TO EAT

There's CKT at every hawker centre and there are mobile carts in or around many of the *kopi tiams*. The below are considered exceptionally good by CKT fiends.

SISTERS CHAR KOAY TEOW
Kopi Kedi Lam Heng, 185 Jalan Macalister, George Town
8.30am-4pm (closed Monday)
The famous sisters have now passed their woks to younger family members; original portraits of the family's grandparents line the walls of this third-generation business. Asian celebrities have graced their tables, and some locals even reckon they can tell the difference between the CKT of each cook. They're so particular about ingredients that the soy sauce is blended to their taste and the prawns and cockles are so fresh they never see a fridge. Their signature is the sprinkling of sweet crabmeat that finishes each plate of CKT. Avoid breakfast time when it's incredibly busy — after 10-ish is a better bet.

PENANG SIAM ROAD CHAR KOAY TEOW
Jalan Siam, opposite Kedai Kopi Hock Ban Hin, George Town
3pm-7pm (closed Monday)
Ask just about anyone in Penang who does the best CKT and to a man they'll say "the old Uncle at Siam Road". Turn up at the Hock Ban Hin coffee shop on the corner of Siam and Anson Roads and wait, with all the other fidgety devotees, for the Uncle to arrive with his cart and ingredients and charge up his charcoal burner, right over the road. There's no exact queuing system and things are a little ad hoc. You place your order with his assistant and wait; during weekend peak times, it can take a full hour for your plate of CKT to arrive. It's worth it. There's such dedication and attention in the way this man cooks, as he fans his flames with a palm-leaf fan and devotedly stir-fries one perfect portion at a time.

TIGER CHAR KWAY TEOW
Kedai Kopi Ping Hooi, 179 Lebuh Carnarvon, George Town
8am-2.30pm, daily
The Yeow family's stall is legendary — locals clamour for the duck egg CKT and love the fact they use bamboo (razor) clams, not blood cockles. Oh and big prawns too and they're generous with the seafood. They set up at the front of the Ping Hooi, an atmospheric old coffee shop — there are about six other hawker stands here so you can graze on a variety of things as well as Tiger's unmissable CKT.

KAFE HENG HUAT
108 Lorong Selamat, George Town
11am-6pm (closed Tuesday)
Penangites once boycotted the red-hatted CKT lady cooking at the cart outside the Heng Huat cafe, on account of her alleged rudeness. But she's busy again so, though undeniably feisty, she's clearly been rehabilitated. She cooks over charcoal, her prawns are meaty, her sausage is melty and her fare has that X-factor that makes it great. Experts rave about her flavours but, at around RM10, hers is one exxy CKT. Be prepared to wait up to 45 minutes during peak times. Also check out the Black Goggle Man cooking CKT outside the Kedai Kopi Dan Ice Kacang at 82 Lorong Selamat. His is very good, although some turn up their noses at his use of gas.

AH LENG
Restoran Tong Hooi, Jalan Dato Keramat, George Town
8.30am-2.30pm (closed Wednesday)
There are a few branches of this famous stall and Ah Leng's children run this one. Their regular plate comes with two big prawns but for around another RM5, you can supersize to deluxe mantis prawns. Duck egg is extra. Their CKT is in hot demand during lunch so come mid-morning to avoid the inevitably tedious wait.

MEE GORENG AT
50-YEAR-OLD
MEE GORENG CRC

Chinese ingredients and technique meet Indian flavouring flair in this island classic; the result is a tasty mess of spiced-up yellow noodles that's a true fusion dish. Also called *'kelinga mee'* or 'Indian' noodles, it originated as a dish sold by itinerant Mamak cooks. It's pure Penang.

MEE GORENG

Pre-cooked yellow wheat noodles are fried in a wok with beansprouts, egg and slices of *tau kwa*, or firm tofu. Seasonings include light and dark soy sauces, chilli sauce, chilli paste and, sometimes, tomato ketchup. Add-ons and garnishes vary from cook to cook but cubes of curried potato, Chinese cabbage, curried squid strips, dried cuttlefish cooked in chilli, and crisp dried prawn fritter (*gneow chu*), either in pieces or served whole on the side, are typical. The same scenario dressed in thick sweet potato and tomato-sauce based gravy is called *mee rebus* and the two dishes are invariably sold from the same places. Both are often garnished with fried shallots, sliced lettuce or sliced green chilli and served with a piece of lime to squirt over. Sometimes beef, mutton or chicken (never pork) are added to the mix. *Mee goreng* makes a satisfying meal at any time of the day although local devotees swear by it for breakfast. ▷

MEE GORENG

Calamansi limes, for garnish

Mee Goreng CRG cook

Cooking at Bangkok Lane

At Hameediyah

Bangkok Lane

Kopi Kedai Ho Ping

WHERE TO EAT

MEE GORENG CRC

Kedai Makanan Seong Huat, 1 Jalan Larut, George Town

1am-4pm (closed Friday)

They're into their third generation of operation and, while the *mee goreng* may appear simple, it packs a punch. It's more Malay than Mamak, which means it's dry, with no saucy gloop. Shreds of mutton or chicken go in, as well as vegetable fritter, tofu and boiled potato. You can have a vegetarian version, or their 'special', with extra bits of squid and tofu.

HUSSAIN MEE GORENG

Jelutong Night Market, Jalan Penaga, George Town

3pm-11pm (closed Friday)

Diehards don't mind venturing down to Jelutong for Hokkien-speaking Hussain's *mee goreng* – he's been tossing noodles over charcoal for some 20 years. These days you're likely to see his son at the stove. They grind their own chilli for sambal, and punters also give the special flavour of Hussain's *mee rebus* gravy a resounding thumbs up.

KOPI KEDAI HO PING

211 Jalan Penang, George Town

8am-9pm (closed Tuesday)

This classic old corner *kopi tiam* is a nice place to watch the word slide by while chomping on some snacks. There's a good *lor bak* (see pg 59) – some say it's the best in downtown G Town. And a great *mee goreng*, spiced with homemade sauce and tinged with that all-crucial *wok hei*.

HAMEEDIYAH

164 Lebuh Campbell, George Town

10.30am-10pm (closed Friday)

They're most famous for their *murtabak* and *biryani* (see pg 40) but gee, while you're at it, you may as well get a *mee goreng* in you. Full of good, spicy tang, the flavour has an old-fashioned honesty, unsurprising given the age of the place (they've been around since 1907). Downstairs is narrow and bustling but the frenzy gives way upstairs to a calm, air-conditioned dining room.

BANGKOK LANE MEE GORENG

Seng Lee Coffee Shop, 270 Jalan Burma, George Town

7am-7pm (closed Wednesday)

Held to be the best *mee goreng* in Penang, this stall is certainly popular. Staffed by a dad and son team, it's been in the family for 90 years and was apparently the first place on the island to cook the dish. They use original family recipes and claim the taste you get now is the same as that from the early 20th century. You're literally eating history!

Little India

Bindis. Burfi. Jalebi and ganeshas. Elegant turbans and swishing saris. Henna-ed hands, wafts of curry, freshly ground spices and the smoke from tandoor ovens. Bollywood hits blaring, colourful jewels gleaming and garlands of bright flowers swinging in the wind. Look around and smell the sandalwood, Toto – you're not in Kansas any more.
Welcome to Little India.

THE SRI
MAHAMARIAMMAN
TEMPLE

AN INDIAN BRIDE
ON HER
WEDDING DAY

LITTLE INDIA

Nagore Durgha shrine, Lebuh Chulia

Detail, Sri Mahamariamman

A Mamak cook,

Indian influence dates back to the earliest days of Penang's British settlement; Francis Light, who founded the colony, notes there were Indian labourers here as early as the 1790s. They were 'Chulias' or people from the Coromandel Coast of the subcontinent and most ended up returning to India with the money they earned. Later, Tamils from around Madras arrived and they were predominantly money lenders – there were effectively no banks in those days so the cash advances they could give to plantation owners and the like helped to kick-start the Penang economy. A later, third wave of immigrants was more permanent than the previous ones; many found work in Malaysia's rubber industry. Today, Indians constitute about 7% of the overall Malaysian population and 10% of Penang's. Their communities in Penang traditionally centred on the Little India enclave which isn't large; it comprises just a few blocks around the Lebuh Pantai (Beach Street) end of Lebuh Chulia.

As well as restaurants, there are shops selling fabrics, cookware, DVDs, clothing, groceries, flowers and dry goods. Tamil is the main dialect spoken although there's Urdu and Punjabi too. Thanks to Penang's religious and ethnic tolerance that began with Francis Light, all aspects of this colourful culture have taken root. You see it in the architecture (note Sri Mahamariamman, one of Penang's oldest Hindu temples), dress, signage, Indian newspapers, vibrant festivals such as Pongal and Deepavali and, naturally, in the food.

Unsurprisingly, given the number of Tamils, many dishes are Southern Indian in origin – banana leaf rice (rice, curries and accompaniments literally served in piles on a large curry leaf; you eat with your hands) and *thosai*, a large, thin rice flour pancake, often seasoned with spices like fenugreek, mustard seeds and cumin, served plain or stuffed, and with side dishes such as *dhal*, are typical. *Poori* (pillowy, deep-fried flat bread served with curry), *idli* (little round steamed, spongy cakes made from fermented rice flour batter, or semolina), *biryani* and *murtabak* (a large, pan-fried filled *roti*) are also common. *Medu vada* are a popular legume-based tiffin snack; they're doughnut-shaped and soft. Then there's *uttapam*, a thick pancake topped with ingredients like onion, tomato, chilli or cabbage, eaten with chutneys and curry gravies. *Nasi kandar* (see pg 76) abounds and many places that sell it are open 24 hours. *Chapatis* and tandoori meats, both northern-derived dishes, are ubiquitous. Mutton, fish, chicken and vegetable curries are easily found and you can get your fix of sweets, such as *gulab jamun*. Little India is a great place for vegetarians and vegans as Southern Indian fare doesn't feature dairy and is light on meat – many dishes don't use it. Coconut is a staple of Tamil cookery, as are turmeric, chillies, tamarind and curry leaves. Northern Indian food employs more dry spices – expect black pepper, cardamom, cinnamon and cloves. ▷

'Mamak' is the name given to Indian Muslims; they are generally of Southern Indian Tamil origin. Both Hindu and Muslim Tamils came to Penang. The Hindus use more vegetables (peas, potato, eggplant, okra, carrot and cabbage, for example) and pulses in their cooking. The Muslims cook a lot of meat, such as mutton, fish, chicken and seafood. Mamak cooking originated on the street with mobile vendors and, while there are still plenty of hawker stands around, some of them spawned full-on restaurants, a few of which are now rather famous. Mamak-run restaurants are halal (no pork) and 'dry' (no beer). Which, depending on how you feel about thirst and the tropics, can be a bit of a bummer if you're not prepared for it. Look for fresh juices, such as watermelon, instead. Typical Mamak dishes include *roti canai* (see pg 14), *teh tarik* ('pulled' tea), *murtabak, thosai, nasi kandar* (see pg 76), *biryani, pasembur* (see pg 59), *naan* with tandoori chicken, and *poori.*▷

CHICKEN *BIRYANI*
AT RESTORAN
KAPITAN

Mutton coconut fry at Dindigul Biryani

Vada

Chapati and curry

Watermelon juice, to cool down a curry

Serving *biryani* rice

Curry spices

Indian Food Decoder

achar: spicy pickle made from vegetables or fruits, served as an accompaniment to curries, breads and snacks

adhirasam: a fried, doughnut-like sweet made from a fermented rice-based batter

apom: a pancake made in concave pans from a rice flour and coconut batter

avial: a thick mix of vegetables (carrot, beans, okra, snake gourd, eggplant etc) cooked with coconut and curry leaves

biryani: rice cooked with a complexity of spices and chicken, seafood, mutton or vegetables; also called *nasi biriani*

chapati: griddle-cooked flat breads made from whole wheat flour; served with curry or dhal as a simple meal

chicken 65: fried, spiced chicken pieces; flavourings can include cayenne, ginger, mustard, vinegar and curry leaves

chicken kali mirch: chicken cooked in a ground black pepper sauce

dal makhani: a Punjabi dish of spiced black lentil and kidney beans, enriched with butter, cream, milk or yoghurt

fish head curry: large fish heads cooked in a curried gravy, also called *kepala ikan*

gulab jamun: fried milk and flour balls soaked in a syrup scented with aromatics like rose, pandan and cardamom

idli: soft, steamed pancakes made from fermented lentils and rice, or semolina, served with chutneys, *dhal* and curry

jalebi: flour batter deep-fried in fine circular shapes, soaked in sugar syrup

jangiri: similar to *jalebi* but but made with a lentil flour batter, then fried in ghee

kothu parotta: shredded flat bread (*parotta* a.k.a. *paratha*) fried with vegetable, egg and spices with curry gravy

murtabak: savoury, stuffed *roti* and a meal in itself. Often filled with minced mutton but vegetables like cabbage are common too – fillings are bound with egg

payasam: rice, tapioca or vermicelli boiled until soft, with milk and sugar. Can be flavoured with raisins, nuts, cardamom or saffron. It's served as a side (it might turn up with your *biryani*!), or as dessert

pongol: a breakfast dish made by boiling rice until very soft; it can be sugared or savoury, seasoned with spices and lentils

poori: a puffed, unleavened fried bread most commonly served for breakfast with curries and chutney

poriyal: a sautéed dish that's usually vegetarian, seasoned with mustard seeds, lentils, onions, chillies, turmeric, coriander and shredded coconut

putu mayam: Sri Lankan string hoppers or fresh rice noodles, often served with coconut and jaggery. Can also be a savoury accompaniment to curries

sambar: a vegetable and lentil stew seasoned with a variety of curry spices

thosai: also spelled '*dosa*', this breakfast staple is a large, thin pancake made from a fermented rice and lentil batter. It's served plain with accompaniments, or stuffed with potatoes (when it's called *masala thosai*) or *paneer*, a curd cheese

uppuma: a porridge-like breakfast dish made from dry roasted semolina with various flavourings (curry leaves, cumin, coconut, mustard seeds, for example)

uttapam: a thick pancake made from a rice and lentil batter. Vegetable toppings, (onion, chilli, cabbage or capsicum) are cooked directly in the batter

vada: a doughnut-shaped fritter made from spiced, mashed lentils, eaten with curry gravies and accompaniments

varuval: a dry meat curry; mutton or chicken are common. Ginger, curry leaves, chilli, cumin, *garam masala* and fennel seeds are typical spices

Idli with accompaniments

A street in Little India

Vada in yoghurt

Gulab jamun and *carrot halwa* at Karaikudi

Burning incense

Fried, spiced chicken '65'

Cooking tandoori chicken

Sweet treats

Garlands of flowers

WHERE TO EAT

RESTORAN KAPITAN
**93 Lebuh Chulia,
George Town
Open 24 hours, daily**
Kapitan pulls in the crowds with its ginormous menu that spans everything from *thosai* to *tandoor*. But their claypot *biryani*, in varieties like quail, chicken, duck, fish, beef and prawn, truly get the juices going. Note they don't serve everything on the menu all day.

THALI NR SWEETS CAFE
**75 Lebuh Penang,
George Town
8am-10pm, daily**
Vegetarian and somewhat nondescript, but don't let the decor put you off. They do a mean *thali*; but the real reason to come is for the Indian sweets. The selection is vast, including *kala jamun* (a dry version of *gulab jamun* stuffed with cashews and raisins), *soan papdi* (a rich, milky square studded with nuts and scented with cardamom), *badam peda* (an almond fudge) and dark and white chocolate *burfi*.

KARAIKUDI RESTAURANT
**20 Lebuh Pasar,
George Town
11am-11pm, daily**
An invitingly cool, dark room sets the scene for some brilliant Southern Indian dining. The chef's signatures include mutton *chukka varuval* (mutton cooked with onion, spices and curry leaves), and the creamy, cashew-rich prawn *malai* curry. Their desserts are pretty – don't miss the dainty *gulab jamun*.

MADRAS NEW WOODLANDS
**60 Lebuh Penang,
George Town
7.30am-11pm, daily**
This strictly vegetarian diner is a local favourite and has an excellent value *thali* for lunch. Called the Woodlands' Special it's an assortment of *chapati, dhal, sambal*, rice, and around five other curry dishes. There's an à la carte menu, and snacks and light dishes to select, buffet style. The freshly-baked *naan*, which they'll optionally serve with butter, is completely yum.

RESTORAN KASSIM MUSTAFA
**Cnr Lebuh Penang and Lebuh Chulia, George Town
Open 24 hours, daily**
With its corner position and splashy green-yellow paint job, you can't miss this place. A favourite since the 1980s, this Mamak eatery has a huge selection of *nasi kandar* dishes (see pg 76). But go for their tender, smoky, tandoori chicken which appears in the afternoon. It's oh so good.

VELOO VILLAS
**22 Lebuh Penang,
George Town
7am-10.30pm (closed Saturday)**
At this small, spick and span banana leaf place, you eat with the locals; it's not particularly touristy. The food is wonderful and the protocol is that you sit, a big piece of banana leaf appears in front of you and servers come and pile on rice and side dishes. Choose white rice or brown, a fried egg and some *sambal*, then either chicken, meat or vegetable curries.

BITE N EAT DINDIGUL BIRYANI
**17 Lebuh Pasar,
George Town
11am-10pm, daily**
Delicious, traditional food served in modern, air-conned surrounds; this is a good choice for travelling families. Portions are generous and flavours, delicious. Try the prawn *biryani*, the *methi murgh masala* (chicken with fenugreek leaves and tomato) and the mutton coconut fry, a dry, peppery dish with spicy oomph.

ALI CAPATI CORNER
**Cnr Lebuh Pasar and Lebuh Queen,
George Town
3pm-9pm (closed every alternate Thursday)**
You'd walk past this if you didn't realise what it is – one of the few places to get *roti jala*, a special, lacy yellow pancake. The runny batter is made from coconut milk, flour and turmeric and the pancakes are formed by artfully dribbling batter on a hot griddle. Order a few, with chicken curry and *teh halia*, or milky ginger tea.

PENANG ROAD
FAMOUS LAKSA

Scrub what you know about *laksa*. This thing is no creamy, dreamy spice bomb – that's *laksa lemak* or Nyonya *laksa*, based on coconut milk. *Assam laksa* is a different beast; it's puckery from tamarind ('*assam*' means sour) and deeply fishy, with an earthy broth that's constructed around mashed-up mackerel.

ASSAM LAKSA

Plenty of punchy ingredients give this soup-noodle dish its very special tang. There's *heh ko*, a type of local prawn paste that's generally served on the spoon you eat the *laksa* broth with. This is in case you don't want to stir it all in; modern tastes have swung against it somewhat. It's strong. Then there's polygonum leaf (a.k.a. Vietnamese mint), lemongrass, *belacan*, turmeric and pretty pink ginger flower (*bunga kantan*), which infuses the soup with a heady, herbal floweriness that's wholly unique. Chopped ginger flower is also used as a raw garnish, along with cooling shreds of cucumber and pineapple, chopped chilli, mint leaves and sliced shallot. When you get a bowl of *assam laksa* in front of you, up wafts a unique complexity of aromas; there's nothing quite like this dish. The noodles used are thickish, round rice noodles and while they're chewy and satisfying, *assam laksa* is really all about the rich broth. ▷

ASSAM LAKSA

The dish is from the Nyonya cooking tradition but it's thought *assam laksa*'s ultimate roots are with the Malays. It can be found all over the place although locals reckon a good one is getting harder to find – many vendors put too much sugar in, use inferior ingredients or skimp on the fish, they reckon. ✤

Fresh nutmeg juice, perfect with *laksa*

Laksa with a side of fried *popiah*

Mint leaves, for garnish

Ginger flowers

Chopped ginger flower is also used as a raw garnish, along with cooling shreds of cucumber and pineapple, chopped chilli, mint leaves and sliced shallot.

WHERE TO EAT

LAKSALICIOUS
123 Jalan Hutton,
George Town
11.30am-7pm (closed Wednesday)
Christine Ooi is raising the bar at her mod little eatery, where the emphasis is on quality ingredients and an updated presentation of classic dishes. She does both an *assam* and a Nyonya (creamy coconut) *laksa* and you can choose your noodles – either thick or thin. Do check out her stylish desserts, such as *sago gula melaka*, made blue with pea flowers and smothered with top-quality palm sugar.

KIM'S LAKSA
Nan Guang Coffee Shop,
67 Jalan Balik Pulau,
Balik Pulau
10am-5pm, Wednesday-Sunday
It's a *laksa*-lover's rite of passage to travel to the southern part of the island for a bowl of Kim's *laksa*. Thick, fishy and moreish, it's best washed down with a deliciously cleansing nutmeg and sour plum juice, made with fresh nutmeg fruits. They make a creamy *laksa* too (here called *Siam laksa*) and you can request a mix of half-half *Siam/assam*.

KEDAI KOPI SIN HWA
329 Jalan Burma,
George Town
10.30am-4.40pm (closed Thursday)
The broth is super chunked-up with mackerel, and

ASSAM LAKSA
the refreshing shreds of cucumber and pineapple are plentiful; go with the locals and order some deep-fried *popiah* to dunk in the soup.

AYER ITAM ASSAM LAKSA
1 Jalan Pasar, Ayer Itam
11.30am-8pm, daily
A famous old hawker stall that's been boiling up *laksa* since 1955. Their soup has a robust, sour flavour from plenty of tamarind and they don't skimp on the fish either. Ayer Itam calls for a taxi jaunt but it's near the famous Kek Lok Si Temple, so you can combine a visit.

PENANG ROAD FAMOUS LAKSA
5 Lebuh Keng Kwee,
George Town
10am-6pm, daily
Famous indeed. *Laksa* lovers make a beeline here, loving this rendition for its sardine and kingfish-based broth, boiled for two hours until the meat completely disintegrates. This stock has heft. For years they were at the nearby Joo Hooi Cafe but have moved further down the lane off Jalan Penang, so don't confuse it.

PENANG ASSAM LAKSA
One Corner Cafe,
4-8 Jalan Bawasah,
George Town
7am-2pm, daily
The daughter of the original Indian Uncle cooks the *assam laksa* now and it's fabulous. This and the other stalls here are beloved by locals. Order some fried crisp *popiah* and use them to mop up the tail end of the *laksa*.

NASI LEMAK
BUNGKUS –
WRAPPED TO-GO,
IN BANANA LEAF

Rice (*nasi*) is a Malay staple; cook it with coconut milk (*santan*) and pandan and you have *nasi lemak*. '*Lemak*' is a word describing creaminess in food, which hints at the gorgeously rich, delicious and moreish flavour of this dish.

NASI LEMAK

Nasi lemak is considered the national dish of Malaysia and is ubiquitous, originating in humble *kampongs* (villages) where coconuts grow abundantly. It's traditionally eaten for breakfast, the cooked rice served with chilli-hot *sambal belacan* (a condiment), crunchy fried *ikan bilis* (tiny dried anchovies) and other accompaniments – a boiled egg, slices of cucumber and a slew of deep-fried peanuts are usual. Each cook has their own recipe for the crucial *sambal*. When the cooked dish is bundled up in a neat banana leaf or paper-wrapped pyramid, designed to grab and go from a hawker stall, it's called '*nasi lemak bungkus*' (*bungkus* means 'wrapped'). There are plenty of restaurants and cafes offering plated, sit-down versions, where the accompaniments can get quite elaborate. Curries, pieces of fried, spiced chicken (*ayam goreng*), beef *rendang*, whole fried or grilled fish and stir-fried *kang kong* (water convolvulus) are examples. ▷

UMAMI TSUNAMI

Stick your snout in a block of this stuff and you'll be smell-shocked from here to kingdom come. Talk about pungent! *Belacan* (say it as 'blat-chan') lies at the heart of Malaysian cooking – it's thought to have appeared around 200 years ago in Malacca and is widely used in curry pastes, sauces, sambals and dressings for dishes like *rojak*. A dark, solid paste that's incredibly odiferous, it's made from fermented shrimp; tiny, krill-like shrimp are steamed, crushed, mixed with salt then left to ferment in the sun. After a few days, they break down to form a coarse, purplish-brown pulp. This is mashed up, compacted into wooden vats then left to ferment some more, before being spread out to dry. The process is repeated until the flavour and texture have matured and the *belacan* is ready to be cut into blocks and packaged. It's often dry-roasted before use, to smooth out the flavour. *Belacan* is a crucial component of *sambal belacan*, which you get with *nasi lemak*. An essential Malaysian condiment, it's made by pounding together, then cooking, *belacan*, chillies, garlic, lime juice and sugar. Penang *belacan* is said to have particularly complex characteristics, due to its long fermentation time. It contains high levels of calcium and protein. ❖

Ali Nasi Lemak

Jin Hoe Cafe

Spicy Lemak

WHERE TO EAT

ALI NASI LEMAK
Sri Weld Food Court,
21 Lebuh Pantai,
George Town
7.30am-4.30pm,
Monday-Friday
In *nasi lemak* terms, this unpretentious stall at the front of the Sri Weld Food Court is Mecca. They still wrap theirs in banana leaves *(duan pisang)* and each day sell hundreds of packets. The parcels are piled on a bench in alphabetised sections, according to fillings; choose between chicken, fried fish, salted fish, prawn, cuttlefish and, their biggest seller, *bilis telur* or anchovies and egg. Watch the lovely owners, Kak Was and Kak Rosni, who are quite used to the attention of food fanatics with cameras, hand-wrapping *nasi lemak* throughout the day.

SPICY LEMAK
177-197 Lebuh Pantai,
George Town
11am-10pm (closed Monday)
The sort of place that old-timers and purists tsk tsk tsk about, Spicy Lemak's schtick is serving rice in three distinct piles, each a different colour. The blue rice is tinted using blue pea flower (see pg 128), the yellow with turmeric, and the striking pink, using dragonfruit juice. While the rice doesn't taste

particularly of coconut, the meals are delicious – order your rice 'set' with a choice of fried chicken (wing or thigh), *sambal*-stuffed grilled fish, prawn and fish or fish curry. Portions are Trump-scale yuge.

KOPITAN CLASSIC
Armenian Street Heritage Hotel, 139 Lebuh Carnarvon, George Town
7.30am-8.30pm, daily
A sanitised, air-conned family option at the base of a hotel, for when you want to play it safe – and dodge the heat outdoors. Right around the corner from Lebuh Armenian, they tint their rice blue with blue pea flower and throw on some crisp, deep-fried wonton skins along with the usual peanuts, *ikan bilis*, egg et al. Good value.

JIN HOE CAFE
46 Jalan Cantonment,
Pulau Tikus
9am-12pm (closed Friday)
This family-run business has been going for 25 years and does a brisk trade in Nyonya-style *nasi lemak*. Side dish choices are simple – either *assam* prawns or grilled fish. The secret is in the home-made *sambal* and the old-fashioned, flavours they achieve. Which some folk reckon are fast disappearing in Penang. The cafe is a taxi ride from central G Town

and is close to Bangkok Lane Mee Goreng (see pg 33) and other hawker outlets.

MEWS CAFE
Muntri Mews Hotel,
77 Jalan Muntri,
George Town
7am-11pm, daily
A lovely boutique hotel with a great little bistro that's like a traditional *kopi tiam*, reimagined. Although upmarket, it's relaxed and unpretentious with a menu offering Western and local dishes. Their version of *nasi lemak* is presented on pretty enamel trays, just one of the many nostalgic touches they employ. Portions are generous and the wait staff are really nice.

PROJEK NASI LEMAK
498 Jalan Dato Keramat,
George Town
12pm-3pm, 6pm-10.30pm (closed Wednesday)
One of the newer wave of *nasi lemak* places, they've upped the presentation game with rectangular white plates and trendy blue coconut rice. There are five different combos of the dish on offer – egg, prawn, squid, chicken or fish set meal. The crisp, deep-fried squid with *nasi lemak* and spicy house *sambal* in particular, get the big thumbs up. You can order extra sides such as *ikan kari* (curry fish) and *sambal* eggplant.

HAWKER STALKER

Roving food hawkers yelling their bill of fare from street to street may no longer be a 'thing' throughout Penang but hawkers are still very much in evidence. They're the heart and soul of the local food scene and are where one turns for some of the island's best, most iconic, dishes. To come to Penang and not eat hawker food is like visiting Giza and giving the pyramids a big swerve. You'd need your head examined.

Food hawkers set up their little mobile carts at *kopi tiams* (coffee shops), on street corners, in food courts, at the side of roads and under trees. There's a concentration of them in the heritage section of George Town but you'll find hawker fare all over the island.

Hawkers inside *kopi tiams* are semi-permanent. Ones on the street appear in the morning or late afternoon, depending on the vendor and, to an extent, the type of food. Hawkers specialise in one or a couple of dishes and some of these, such as *chee cheong fun*, are more evident in the morning while others, like *lok lok* (see pg 108), are evening dishes. Then there are permanent hawker centres, some quite large. The food is always cheap (cash only) and delicious; note that in a hawker centre or *kopi tiam*, it's generally mandatory to buy a drink in order to occupy a seat. In food-crazed Penang everyone has a preferred hawker vendor and endless opinions percolate as to why/how/what makes his/her fav dish of X/Y/Z the ultimate/best ever/el supremo. Chasing 'the best' becomes exhausting so don't get hung up on quests for the ultimate version of a dish. Just eat. You won't go wrong. ▷

A BOWL
OF CURRY MEE

53

1. ROJAK

2. ANG TAU TH'NG

3. POPIAH

4. OH CHIEN

5. CHEE CHEONG FUN

6. PAO

7. BAN CHIEN KUEH

8. BAK KUT TEH (DRY)

9. SIEW BAK

10. CURRY MEE

11. NASI GORENG

12. CHAR KOAY KAK

13. SATAY

14. PASEMBUR

15. LOH MEE

16. LAM MEE

17. AIS TINGKAP

18. WAN TAN MEE

19. LOR BAK

20. OR KUIH

Essential Hawker Dishes

1. ROJAK: salad of underripe fruits and crisp vegetables in a thick, sweet, prawn paste sauce
Hock Seng Rojak King, Gat Lebuh Cecil, George Town, 1pm-6pm, daily

2. ANG TAU TH'NG: red bean pudding (a Chinese-style dessert) served hot or cold
Kopi Kedai Sin Guat Keong, Lebuh Kimberley, George Town, 6pm-late (closed Monday)

3. POPIAH: a fat, fresh spring roll filled with seasoned tofu, yam bean, egg, lettuce
Stall 17, Padang Brown, Jalan Perak, George Town, 2pm-7pm (closed Thursday)

4. OH CHIEN: fried oyster omelette; there are two versions, one sticky, the other crisp
Kedai Kopi Lam Ah, 194 Lebuh Pantai, George Town, 10.30am-4.30pm (closed Sunday)

5. CHEE CHOENG FUN: rolled sheets of fresh, soft rice noodle served with thick, sweetened prawn paste and chilli sauce
Seow Fong Lye Cafe, 94 Lorong Macalister, George Town, 7.30am-12.30pm, daily

6. PAO: steamed, Chinese-style yeast buns with various sweet or savoury fillings
Sri Weld Food Court, Lebuh Pantai, George Town, 9am-5pm, daily

7. BAN CHANG KUIH: a thick, spongy pancake cooked over coals, filled with peanuts, sugar and margarine, or corn, peanut and egg
Cnr Jalan Kuala Kangsar and Lebuh Kimberley, George Town, 7.30am-11am, daily

8. BAK KUT TEH: pork braised in a spiced, medicinal soup; there's also a dry type
Coffee Island, 77 Persiaran Gurney, George Town, 7am-2am, daily

9. SIEW BAK: Chinese-style roast pork with noodles, complete with very crisp skin
Wai Kee, 348 Lebuh Chulia, George Town, 11.30am-2.30pm (closed Sunday)

10. CURRY MEE: spiced, coconut milk-based soup noodles topped with curried dried squid, pork blood cubes and tofu
Sisters Curry Mee, Jalan Paya Terubong, Ayer Itam, 7.30am-1pm (closed Tuesday)

11. NASI GORENG: spicy, Javanese-style fried rice, often topped with fried egg
Gurney Drive Hawker Centre (see details Where to Eat, pg 61)

12. CHAR KOAY KAK: rice flour cubes fried with dark soy sauce, radish, egg and sprouts
Sister Yao's Char Koay Kak, Lorong Macalister, George Town, 7am-1pm, daily

13. SATAY: marinated bits of meat (pork or chicken, usually) grilled on skewers over charcoal, served with peanut sauce
New Lane Hawker Centre (see details Where to Eat, pg 61)

14. PASEMBUR: shredded raw vegetables, cubes of potato and tofu, slices of fried fritter and seafood (you choose from a selection) in a thick, sweet-spicy sauce
Kareem Pasembur Rojak, Lebuh Union, George Town, 11am-6pm, daily

15. LOH MEE: noodles in dark broth thickened with tapioca flour, with egg, fried shallot, pork or chicken, chilli and garlic pastes; popular for breakfast
Kedai Kopi Seng Thor, 160 Lebuh Carnarvon, George Town, 2pm-5pm, daily

16. LAM MEE: noodles in pork-prawn stock with egg, prawns, pork and fried shallot
Campbell Street Market, Lebuh Campbell, George Town, 7am-12pm, daily

17. AIS TINGKAP: a rose-flavoured drink originating in Penang, featuring young coconut and basil seeds, infused with herbs
Ais Tingkap, Lebuh Tamil, George Town, 11am-7pm (closed Sunday)

18. WAN TAN MEE: wan tan with fresh noodles, pork and vegetable garnishes, in soup. There is also a dry version, in dark soy sauce; wan tans may be served fried
Chulia Street Wantan Mee, Cnr Lebuh Chulia & Carnarvon, George Town, 6pm-10pm, daily

19. LOR BAK: minced meat or veg, seasoned with five-spice powder, wrapped in beancurd skin and deep fried; served with chilli sauce
Kafe Kheng Pin, 80 Jalan Penang, George Town, 7am-3pm, daily

20. OR KUIH: savoury steamed taro cake, topped with dried shrimp and fried shallot
Eng Loh Kopitiam, 48 Lebuh Gereja, George Town, 8am-3pm (closed Sunday)

HAWKER STALKER

A food hawker at his wok

Chee cheong fun

Dry version of wan tan mee

At Lorong Macalister

WHERE TO EAT

GURNEY DRIVE HAWKER CENTRE
172 Solok Gurney, 1 Pulau Tikus, George Town
4pm-12am, daily
Situated along the famous seafront promenade, this fills nightly with food lovers. With its festooned lights and happy vibes, dining here is bound to become a highlight. You'll find a satisfying range of dishes, from *satay*, *char koay teow*, *Hokkien mee*, *nasi goreng* and *pasembur* to *rojak*. There's a halal section too.

NEW LANE HAWKER CENTRE
Lorong Baru, George Town
4pm-2am, daily
The street closes to traffic every afternoon, allowing hawkers to set up shop; you sit at tables on the curb in the open air. There's so much to eat – *chee cheong fun*, curry mee, oh chien, grilled fish, *koay kak*, *koay teow th'ng*, laksa, popiah, congee and *wan tan mee*, for starters. The cooking action is great, with plenty of woks hissing, fires flaming and burners smoking. A local favourite with a less touristy atmosphere; find it at the Macalister end of Lorong Baru.

PRESGRAVE STREET HAWKER CENTRE
67A Lebuh Presgrave, George Town
4.30pm-12.30am, Friday-Wednesday
Where do the locals dine? At places like this little enclave of hawker stalls. There's the legendary *Hokkien mee* (see pg 62) and there's also duck egg *char koay teow*, *ice kacang* and *cendol*, *oh chien*, *lo bak* and *wan tan mee*, for example.

NEW WORLD PARK FOOD COURT
102 Jalan Burma, George Town
10am-9pm, daily
Undercover and with about 20 stalls, this permanent food court is spruce. It's well ventilated, with a soaring canopy roof and modern feel – perfect for when you want less smoke and argy bargy with your dinner. The curry mee lady is popular, as are the guys selling meat dumplings and steamed taro cake. There's also *assam laksa*, *ice kacang*, a pretty *rojak* with the sauce on the side and sweet, red bean dessert.

LEBUH KIMBERLEY
George Town
5pm-11pm (approx), daily
Early in the evening, downtown George Town (around the corner of Cintra and Kimberley) officially becomes Gorge Town. There's already a thick slew of *kopi tiams* and carts, including the Bee Hooi Coffee Shop, but at night the food options swell. *Lok lok*, soy sauce duck, traditional Chinese desserts, satay, *char koay teow*, fried *bee hoon* (noodles)... this precinct really goes off.

CECIL STREET MARKET
40-48 Lebuh Cecil, George Town
7am-7pm, daily
Around for yonks, this is one of the largest hawker centres in George Town. It houses a wet market as well, attracting a steady stream of locals. There's a mammoth selection of dishes: *pasembur*, Nyonya *kuih*, *lor bak*, *jawa mee* (sour-spicy soup noodles), *koay teow th'ng*, curry mee, roast meats, *otak otak* and *popiah*. Plus hard-to-find gems like *loh mai chee*, peanut and sugar-stuffed sticky rice dough that's deep-fried until golden. And jelly-like savoury fried sago (*sago char*), seasoned with dark soy sauce.

JALAN CHOWRASTA,
1-33 Jalan Chowrasta, George Town
7.30am-early afternoon (approx), daily
The streets around Chowrasta Bazaar are a trove of food stalls, *kopi tiams* and fresh fruit, cake, fish, poultry, meat and snack vendors. Food lovers, do not miss it. About half way up Jalan Chowrasta, tucked off the street, is a small hawker precinct. You'll find *char koay kak*, which isn't as common as other hawker offerings, *lam mee* and other goodies. It's less frenetic here than most hawker enclaves and is an excellent option in the morning for breakfast.

*HOKKIEN MEE
FOR BREAKFAST IN
GEORGE TOWN*

Ah, *Hokkien mee*. Surely it's *the* defining taste of Penang, served in a brimming bowl. The secret's in the broth, long-cooked with pork bones and given plenty of prawny oomph by the inclusion of prawn shells, heads and all their tasty goo.

HOKKIEN MEE

Rich and burnished brown-red in colour, aromatic and bursting with flavour, a good *Hokkien mee* broth should be a touch spicy with a slightly sweet edge. Every vendor puts their own mark on it; some versions have more chilli heat, others more prawn intensity and others, thicker broth.

The dish has altered a little over the years; these days it's usual, for example, for it to be served with boiled egg, a complete heresy to purists. As well as the soup, there are noodles, customarily a mix of *mee* (yellow egg noodles) and *bee hoon* (dried rice vermicelli) although you can also have just one or the other. Beansprouts and a little *kang kong* (water convolvulus) go in the bowl too, and garnishes of pork slices, fried shallots and cooked prawns. Sometimes there'll be a scatter of fried lard cubes or slices of pig skin and some vendors, for extra dosh, offer add-ons like pork ribs, pieces of crackling-topped roast pork or extra prawns. ▷

HOKKIEN MEE

There's always a spoon of chilli paste to stir in and give the whole thing a big kick in the spice pants.

A classic hawker dish, you find *Hokkien mee* (also called prawn *mee* and *har mee*) all over the island, at every time of the day – it's especially popular for breakfast. Vendors make their broth well in advance so when they set up, all they need to do is get it simmering, get ready a noodle blanching station, have all the garnishes at hand and boom. You're fed. The dish is unique to Penang; if you go, for example, to KL and ask for *Hokkien mee*, you'll get a stir-fried noodle dish (called *Hokkien char*) that's nothing like this. ✤

888 Hokkien Mee

888 Hokkien Mee

Ping Hooi Cafe

Hokkien refers to a dialect group from Fujian province in southern China. **Teochew** (also spelled Chiuchow) is another dialect group but from eastern Guangdong province in China. As well as language, each group has particular culinary styles which are the main two Chinese cuisines in Penang.

WHERE TO EAT

888 HOKKIEN MEE
67A Lebuh Presgrave,
George Town
5pm-11.45pm (closed
Tuesday)
This is the prawn mee
against which all others
are judged; the stock is
gutsy, the portion big
and you can customise
your toppings by adding
fish balls, pork ribs, pork
belly or pork leg. Expect
daunting queues – but
they move fast. (BTW in
the morning, there's an
excellent Hokkien mee
stall right over the road,
from 8am to 12pm).

CY CHOY ROAD
HOKKIEN MEE
533 Jalan CY Choy,
George Town
7am-2.30pm (closed
Sunday)
The cook is over 70
and he makes a stock
that's clearer, lighter and
somehow 'fresher' tasting
than others. He's generous
with fried shallots and you
can ask for some pork
rib in your soup. Experts
recommend laying off the
accompanying chilli paste
so as not to ruin the bright
flavours of the broth.

CIFU OMAR @ KAFE
GOODALL
6L Jalan Tanjung
Tokong, Seri Tanjung
10am-2pm, daily
Chef Omar's halal
version of Hokkien mee
has many fans. As well
as prawns and boiled

HOKKIEN MEE
egg, you get crabmeat,
shredded chicken and,
if you're not chicken, the
bird's gizzards. Omar's
in a food court with many
other dining options.

OLD GREEN HOUSE
PRAWN MEE
149 Jalan Burma,
George Town
9.30am-3.30pm, daily
As if their big bowls of
Hokkien mee weren't
enough, you can 'kah
liu' or 'add extras' –
everything from pork
belly to Chinese sausage,
chicken's feet, pork
intestines and prawns.

AH SOON KOR
HAR MEE
169 Lebuh Carnarvon,
George Town
7am-1pm (closed
Wednesday)
Despite the accepted
superiority of their broth,
it's the add-ons that lure.
There's the usual spare
ribs, roasted pork and
extra prawns, plus deep-
fried mantis prawns. Their
special chilli paste is home
made and not as belacan-
heavy as elsewhere.

PING HOOI CAFE
179 Lebuh Carnarvon,
George Town
6.30am-5pm, daily
A solid choice in central
George Town. The old
kopi tiam is atmospheric,
with a number of hawker
dishes on offer besides
a dependable Hokkien
mee. Including, in the
mornings, duck egg char
koay teow (see pg 24).

George Town

When you've *jelak makan*, or 'eaten too much rich food', it's time to stretch your legs, look up and take in the vintage structures. Penang's architectural heritage is astounding, with weathered cemeteries, quaint cinemas, monuments, clan temples, pre-war shophouses, crumbling old hotels and colonial mansions thick on the ground.

A TYPICAL VIEW OF GEORGE TOWN'S LONG NARROW SHOPHOUSES

Entire streets — nay, blocks — possess charming authenticity, with many places a bit crusty, creaky and peeling from decades of use. Things are not, refreshingly, overly tarted up for tourism. Yet (#dontgochanging). While the entire, UNESCO-listed kit and caboodle is worthy, here are a few locales to zero in on. And some dining advice at the end, for when you're ready to *makan* big again.

THE OLD
PROTESTANT
CEMETERY

OLD PROTESTANT CEMETERY

Jalan Sultan Ahmad Shah, George Town

One of the oldest cemeteries in Malaysia, the earliest grave is dated 1789. The place is mostly deserted, and the graves moss-covered and weathered. Reading headstones is a fascinating way to spend an hour or so. Francis Light, who claimed Penang for England, is buried here, as is Thomas Leonowens, the husband of Anna Leonowens, of *The King And I* fame.

CLAN JETTIES

Pengkalan Weld, George Town

This series of rickety wooden jetties is where impoverished Chinese immigrants and their extended families, working at the port or as fishermen, built humble homes and temples over the water. Six jetties survive – the oldest and largest is the Chew jetty, dating from the mid-19th century. Newer ones, like the Pen Aung (now demolished) and Mixed Clan jetties, were established in the 1960s. Today, some dwellers have opened souvenir shops and other tourist-related businesses to keep, er, afloat. It's interesting to know that jetty dwellers don't have to pay tax as, technically, they don't live on land.

CHEONG FATT TZE MANSION

14 Lebuh Leith, George Town

Also called The Blue Mansion on account of its striking paint job, this was built between 1896 and 1902 by craftsmen brought from China. Cheong Fatt Tze was a Chinese who made his fortune from coffee, rubber and tea; he became one of the richest men in South-East Asia. Bucking the trend to build in the European

Cheong Fatt Tze Mansion

Chinese cake

Steamed pandan cakes

One of the old Clan Jetties

style, his place is gloriously and resolutely Chinese, albeit with Western flourishes (note the Scottish cast iron, Frenchy louvred windows and English floor tiles). Its 38 rooms, five courtyards and seven stairways are home to a boutique hotel and restaurant – you can book a public tour and have a squizz, if you're not staying there.

BEACH STREET

In George Town's commercial heart and parallel to the coastline, Beach Street (now called Lebuh Pantai) is one of George Town's oldest, grandest streets. It's lined with architectural gems that were once banks, company headquarters, trading societies and the like. Look for the old Netherlands Trading Society building at No 9, which still retains its original 1905 appearance. And No 32-34, built in 1886, with lovely cast-iron balconies on the second floor; this is the oldest building on the street to still preserve its original appearance. India House (originally the US Information Service Library) with its elephant head embellishment, and the old George Town Dispensary at No 39, are also mighty handsome.

NAGORE DURGHA SHRINE

Cnr Lebuh King and Lebuh Chulia
Lebuh Chulia is another of George Town's oldest streets, with landmark buildings and points of interest. Including the oldest Indian Muslim shrine in Penang, built in 1803 and commemorating a 13th-century saint from Nagore in India. Not far away is the 1870 Han Jiang Ancestral Temple, with an ornate gate, beautifully painted front doors and other decorative features.

Posing on George Town's street art trail

Cake at De Tai Tong

WE SERVE ALL TYPE OF CHINESE CUISINE & DELICASES INCLUDING NOODLES

各类 小炒
特色 小菜
炒粉 面食
无 任选延

THE LEE JETTY, ONE
OF SIX CLAN JETTIES,
LIT UP AT NIGHT

ANTIQUE TEA SET
AND MOON CAKE
MOULDS IN A
GEORGE TOWN SHOP

CITY HALL

Jalan Padang Kota Lama

Although built in 1903, this wasn't called City Hall until city status was conferred on George Town by Queen Elizabeth II in 1957 (it was Malaysia's first official city). A gorgeous old pile with Palladian and Edwardian Baroque elements, it was the first building in Penang to have electric lights, and people would come to gaze at it, lit up after dark.

ST GEORGE'S CHURCH

1 Lebuh Farquhar
10am-4pm, Monday-Thursday

Consecrated in 1819, this was declared a National Treasure in 2007. Its elegant steeple and columned portico dominate a large green space; it was constructed using Indian convict labour. The 1886 pavilion was erected to memorialise Francis Light. You can attend Sunday services (check the board for times). Keep walking along Lebuh Farquhar until you come to the Penang State Museum, in a striking 1896 building that was originally a school.

MASJID KAPITAN KELING

14 Jalan Buckingham
1pm-5pm, Saturday-Thursday,
3pm-5pm, Friday

One of the island's most notable buildings, this mosque was built in 1801 by Indian Muslim traders, and greatly enlarged in the 1930s. The spectacular onion-shaped dome and pitched roof are part of the original structure.

PARAMOUNT HOTEL

48F Jalan Sultan Ahmad Shah

Here's a time warp if ever there was one. They still register guest names on hand-

Lebuh Campbell

Masjid Kapitan Keling

Dim sum at Yong Pin

annotated cards, slotted into a rack on the wall. Upstairs, huge rooms are decked out à la the 40s and 50s. The hotel is down a drive off Jalan Sultan Ahmad Shah where, despite the development, there are some incredible old mansions, some crumbling and neglected, others not.

CAMPBELL STREET MARKET

Cnr Lebuh Campbell and Lebuh Buckingham

A small community wet market built in 1900 and looking completely untouched since then. It's rumoured to have been built on the site of an old Malay cemetery and it's said that stall holders had to be convinced to tenant it. Some still insist it's haunted, claiming they see ghosts wafting about in the small hours. Woooooo...

KHOO KONGSI

18 Cannon Square, George Town

A clan temple built in the grandest of styles, it's one of the largest in Malaysia. Until WWII it was basically a self-contained village for the Khoo Clan, complete with its own educational, welfare and social organisations. It's located in one of the oldest sections of George Town and surrounded by quaint and winding lanes.

WISMA KASTAM BUILDING

Cnr Weld Quay and Gat Lebuh China

Built in 1909 by the Federated Malay States Railways, the clock tower was, in its day, the tallest structure in Penang. Used originally for railway administration offices, this is where train tickets were once booked – back then, passengers had to be ferried to the mainland where the trains were boarded.

Did you know?

+ Popular street Love Lane supposedly got its name as it was where wealthy Straits Chinese, living along nearby Muntri Lane, kept their mistresses.

+ George Town was named after King George III of England and is the birthplace of Jimmy Choo, the celebrated shoe designer.

+ In 2012, Lithuanian artist Ernest Zacharevic created six wall paintings depicting local culture that have become part of George Town's famous street art scene. The most famous is the *Children on Bicycle*, on Armenian Street.

+ George Town was once the centre of Malaysia's print media.

+ Sun Yat-Sen held a famous meeting on Armenian Street that led to the 1911 downfall of the Chinese Qing Dynasty.

+ Many of the original Penang street names have been changed, although old timers still refer to their colonial names. FYI ...'*jalan*' means 'road', '*lebuh*' means 'street', '*persiaran*' means 'drive', '*lorong*' means 'lane', '*pengkalan*' means 'quay', '*medan*' means 'square' and '*lebuhraya*' means 'avenue'.

WHERE TO EAT

You're not exactly stuck for choice in George Town with *kopi tiams*, hawker carts, traditional bakeries and venerable old restaurants thick on the ground. As well as the plethora of options mentioned elsewhere in this book, consider these:

TEK SEN
18 Lebuh Carnarvon,
George Town
12pm-2.30pm, 6pm-8.30pm (closed Tuesday)
Considered by many to be the best Chinese-style restaurant in town, this started as a humble stall in 1965. Occupying a pair of shophouses, there's nothing in the stripped-back interior to divert from the food; twice-cooked pork in *chilli padi*, a sweet-sticky fry up that's chewy and incredibly rich, is their signature. Dishes come in three sizes, handy for couples or solo diners, while groups can order up big.

DE TAI TONG
45 Lebuh Cintra,
George Town
6am-2.30pm,
6.15pm-11.30pm, daily
Old-school dim sum offered from rattly trolleys by smiling (usually) Aunties, food here will fill you up quick-smart. It gets packed at peak times but come early enough in the morning, and you'll secure a curb-side table where

you can slurp tea with the regulars.

ENG AUN KOPITIAM
Cnr Lebuh Kimberley and Jalan Kuala Kangsar,
George Town
7am-12pm, Wednesday-Sunday
A character-filled coffee shop that's one of many; the quiet-ish corner location, the food vendors just outside, and its proximity to Chowrasta Bazaar make it an ideal place to get down with the locals. They brew a mean coffee and the kitchen puts out Chinese-style dishes, such as pork knuckle noodles and stewed chicken's feet.

THO YUEN RESTAURANT
92 Lebuh Campbell,
George Town
6am-3pm (closed Tuesday)
The ladies are lovely, and eager to see you fill up on their yum cha and congee for breakfast; later in the day there's chicken rice, *chai boey* (a stew of leftover meat, preserved mustard leaves and tamarind) and *hong tu* noodles (deep-fried noodles served in a sturdy, eggy soup). It's said their egg tarts are the best in George Town.

YONG PIN RESTAURANT
11 Jalan Sungai Ujong,
George Town
6am-12pm, 7pm-12am,
daily
Another nostalgic dim sum place, open since the 1980s. There are familiar staples: *siu mai*, sticky rice,

spare ribs and fish balls. Check out the century egg, deep-fried in beancurd skin, and the fried water chestnut cake for dessert. There are plenty of good noodle dishes and on Friday and Saturday, their top-selling braised ginger duck noodles (*yee foo mee*) makes a welcome appearance.

HIM HEANG CAKE SHOP
162 Jalan Burma,
George Town
8.30am-5pm (closed Sunday)
This family-run enterprise, where all the biscuits are handmade, started up three generations ago. They're credited with inventing the *tambun* biscuit, a smaller version of the famous *tau sar pneah*, a pastry ball with a green bean filling. It can be either sweet or salty. Plenty of other places in George Town make them, and derivative versions — pandan ones are popular.

JAWI HOUSE CAFE
85 Lebuh Armenian,
George Town
11am-10pm (closed Tuesday)
Here's a little known fact: there are Indian Peranakans. It's a small group though and to get a sense of their cuisine, or to just eat darned well, head here for delicious food lovingly cooked; try herbal *lemuni* rice and refreshing mango salad. Proprietor Dr Wazir Jahan Karim is a respected culinary author.

AT RESTORAN
ROS MUTIARA IN
LITTLE INDIA

Here's a dish that food styling forgot. There's not much that's pretty about a fully-loaded plate of *nasi kandar*, a total shambles of curry-saturated rice, chicken, fish, prawn, egg or whatever else you've got heaped on your serve.

NASI KANDAR

But what's lacking in Instagram-friendly looks is more than made up for in the mountains of full-on flavour. If you like curry spice, this is your dish; many *nasi kandar* specialists still mix their own spice combinations. Synonymous with Penang (people say it tastes so good here because the local water is sweet), *nasi kandar* originated with Indian Muslim food vendors. It gets its name from the *kandar*, a type of shoulder pole; street vendors once balanced big buckets of hot curry and rice on a pole and carried them around, hawking on the streets. Theirs was hearty food for coolies and the curries were simple, rugged and home cooked. Nowadays, there are plenty of restaurants devoted to *nasi kandar* and some of these cook as many as 50 or 60 dishes to eat with the rice. Technically, many of these dishes blur the lines between Malay and Indian cuisines, creating a culinary mash-up that's enjoyed by all of Penang's ethnic groups. ▷

NASI KANDAR

To order, you line up at the service area where there'll be a clutter of pots, platters of fried bits and steamed things, plus large dishes of braises, stews and spicy stir fries. Choosing can be a little overwhelming. A server heaps rice on your plate, then you point to what you want on it: steamed okra, fried chicken, some curried squid, liver, quail, fish roe or prawns, stir-fried cabbage or bitter gourd, or salted egg, for example. There will be dry curries, such as *rendang*; sweet and sour dishes; coconut milk-sauced vegetables; meat, seafood or vegetable *sambals*; and 'ketchup' dishes, i.e. cooked in sweet, thick soy sauce. There's no pork as this meal is halal. Rice is often served from a tall, cylindrical wooden container which is supposed to enhance its flavour.

Nasi Z Benua Koo Boo Cafe

Once you've chosen a few chunks of good-looking protein and other bits and bobs, over go the curry gravies (called *kuah*) and this is the true genius of *nasi kandar*. There's an art to this 'flooding' (called 'banjir') of your plate with gravy – it's not just about making a mess, even though it totally looks that way. Four or five gravies, each from a different pot, go over your meal in an act that's part dance, part ladling; the gravyologist swirls, blobs, dribbles and gloops the sauces over everything, finishing with a long-armed flourish. The expertise is in the mixing of the many flavours – there might be beef, chicken and fish-derived curry sauces all mooshed together but somehow, they work. Flavours are explosive and portions can be massive; you pay according to what's on your plate and it's very easy for hungry eyes to be larger than hungry stomachs.

Many places open 24 hours, and *nasi kandar* is as popular for breakfast as it is for lunch or dinner. Some diners opt to have their curry gravies in separate dishes at the table, especially when sharing. You'll also see menu boards touting 'nasi dalcha' where the rice is cooked with lentils or *dhal* and vegetables. Although you don't have to, it's customary to eat *nasi kandar*, and other Mamak dishes, with your hands. Which brings us to...

Dishing up gravies

At Line Clear

Eating with hands at Restoran Deen

...how to eat with your hands

1. Wash those mitts first
It seems a bit parental to state it but there you go. *Nasi kandar* places have plenty of sinks dotted about for this purpose.

2. Use your right hand only!
In Muslim circles the left hand is reserved for, er, other stuff. Wiping. You know where and what. (Sorry, Lefties.)

3. Appraise that plateful
Determine where all the solid, big things like chicken or whole prawns lurk. These are easy to tackle and can be used to scoop. Loose and small stuff is harder.

4. Use the tips of your thumb and forefingers to nudge a mouthfuls-worth of rice to the side of your plate. Work it into as much of a compact ball as you can, then form your fingers into a scoop shape. Lower your face over your plate and deftly shovel that scoops-worth of food into your mouth. Some may tumble down your sleeve but no worries. You're new to this.

5. Tear off bits of chicken, mutton or whatever else is solid and use these to fortify your mounds of rice and render them more stable on their way to your gob.

6. Remember this sequence – scoop, lift and dump (in that mouth. Not down your shirt). Do this quickly and determinedly. Prevaricating or otherwise messing around means, well, mess.

7. Use your left hand for your can or glass of drink.

8. If there's naan or chapati about, use pieces of that to scoop up food; it makes life easier.

9. If it doesn't work out, it's ok to grab a fork and spoon
NO judgment. At all. (Wuss!)

TYPICAL SELECTION
OF *NASI*
KANDAR DISHES

WHERE TO EAT

Note that many places listed in Little India (see pg 34) also serve *nasi kandar*.

RESTORAN DEEN MAJU
170 Jalan Gurdwara, George Town
5am-4pm, 5pm-4am, daily
Enormous queues are the order of the day here but they move quickly. Many punters go for a chunk of the *ayam goreng* (fried chicken) or *ayam kicap* (chook cooked in sweet soy sauce), and for good reason: they're delicious. Grilled squid, salted egg, fish roe with curry gravy or the *kuah campur* (mixed gravy) are all great.

NASI KANDAR LINE CLEAR
177 Jalan Penang, George Town
Open 24 hours
Maybe the most famous and oldest of the *nasi kandar* joints, they're used to newbies and the friendly guys will help you choose your dishes. They'll likely steer you to their famous fish head curry and do go with it – the tender cheek meat is sublime. Daily specials are worth checking out; above all, be prepared for gargantuan portions.

LIYAQAT ALI NASI KANDAR
98 Jalan Masjid Kapitan Keling, George Town
10pm-9am, daily
One for the night owls

with its evening hours; this place is colloquially known as 'Queue Up Nasi Kandar' which hints at its popularity. It's wedged into an alleyway next to the Kapitan Keling mosque, where it's been since 1943. Their recipes, they say, haven't changed over the years and locals love their beef curry in black sauce, and chicken curry where the meat is marinated in spices and fried before going into the gravy. A glass of icy rose syrup is the perfect accompaniment.

RESTORAN ROS MUTIARA
128 Lebuh Chulia, George Town
Open 24 hours
"If good tell your friends, if not tell us" is their motto. They're chirpy here – sit at one of the front tables and you'll be in the midst of the *nasi kandar*-serving and *bee hoon*-frying action. On a corner right opposite the ever-popular Kapitan restaurant (see pg 43), it's handy to all the other Little India action too.

NASI 7 BENUA KOO BOO CAFE
Taman Tunas Muda, Bayan Lepas
11.30am-11pm (closed Sunday)
'Nasi 7 Benua' means 'the rice of seven continents' and you do, in fact, get seven pert little mounds of perfectly moulded rice that look like ping pong balls. Each is a different colour

and they look too beautiful to drown in curry gravy. There's plain rice, tomato rice, coconut rice, *lemuni* rice (coloured deep grey with *lemuni* leaves, used for their flavour and medicinal benefits), green *kacang* rice (with lentils), yellow *nasi minyak* ('oil' rice) and *nasi hujan* or 'rainbow' rice. The curries are spicy-tasty and they offer bottomless, free iced tea. A bit out of the main thrust of George Town but worth checking out.

SUP HAMEED
48 Jalan Penang, George Town
Open 24 hours
Another famous outlet, known for their fiery flavours – and a big selection of vegetable as well as meat dishes, sometimes a welcome respite after eating loads of flesh. Expect things like green beans in soy sauce, steamed okra and a mixed vegetable curry. Make sure you get some of the greenish coconutty *kurma* gravy over your rice.

RESTORAN TAJUDDIN HUSSAIN
49-51 Lebuh Queen, George Town
11am-3.30pm, 6.30pm-10pm (closed Sunday)
Located on the edge of Little India, this unassuming place is very much a local hangout and boy, it gets busy. The milky-pale mutton *korma* and *ayam ros* (a rich, red chicken curry) are delishimo.

BONELESS, SOY SAUCE
DUCK WITH TOFU
AND EGG

Eeny, meeny, miny moe. Catch some poultry by the toe. If it squawks … no wait. Duck or chook? Soy sauce braised, or poached? Roasted, with crisp skin? Breast or thigh? Bones in or out? Oh shoot, let's consider the whole, birdified shebang shall we; it's too hard to choose.

DUCK RICE

Indeed, eating poultry with steamed rice, a few simple garnishes and a light lick of sauce is one of Penang's great, unsung dining experiences. It's easily overlooked in favour of the island's more spiced-up offerings but there's something deliciously soothing about soft, juicy bird flesh eaten with some properly cooked rice. Whether poached, steamed, braised or roasted, these simple dishes speak to the significant Southern Chinese influence on the local culinary repertoire.

The best roast duck places prepare their ducks according to guarded family processes; some are into their fourth generation. Famous outlets draw salivating devotees way before the cooked ducks arrive – invariably on the back of a scooter. Then, it's a flurry of chopping, slicing and incising those birds, until the last skerrick of juicy meat is gone. At these places, you'll also see chunks of *char siew* (BBQ pork), *siew bak* ▷

DUCK RICE

(roast pork) and delicious roasted chicken too; you can mix and match your proteins, to taste. The roast ducks, dangling by their necks on hooks, are said to look a bit like a *pipa*, a pear-shaped Chinese lute. This similarity gives the dish its local Chinese name – *pei pa* duck.

Takeaway at Fatty Loh

Then, there's soy sauce duck, a lip-smacking dish of bird simmered to a mahogany hue in a spice-infused soy sauce mix – you'll also see wings, feet, intestines, duck eggs and other duck bits cooked this way. What it lacks in roasted, crunchy skin, soy sauce duck more than makes up for in silky-textured flesh, properly laminated with lush fat. There's a chicken equivalent too, and most places feature both birds on their menus; again, you can order half-half. Their service is simple; you say how much bird you want, it goes over rice with a ladleful of rich, brown sauce with chilli sauce on the side. A bowl of *chai boey* soup, literally made using leftover meaty bits, preserved mustard greens and tamarind, is a good accompaniment.

Hainan chicken rice at Kim Poh

There's no duck equivalent of Hainan chicken. Cooked by carefully steeping the whole bird in stock, the flesh finishes up the purest white and is extremely juicy; it's an art to get just the right succulence and texture. The rice is cooked in the chicken stock and has a slight, fatty richness; for this reason it's called 'oil' rice. Chilli sauce to dip, a bit of soy, maybe a few garnishes like cucumber slices and bada bing! That's it. ❖

Soy sauce and Hainan chicken

WHERE TO EAT

**FATTY LOH
CHICKEN RICE**
21 Jalan Fettes, Tanjung Tokong
9.30am-6pm, daily
The most hyped chicken rice on the island, Fatty's has been a fixture for decades. Dubbed 'The King of Chicken Rice', they've been plying their trade for more than 30 years. The current location, with its quirky antique decor, is atmospheric. The menu encompasses roast and Hainan-style chicken, with the choice of specific cuts like breast, thigh or leg. There's duck too, either braised or roasted, and other dishes if you want to venture into, say, pork territory. The best place to sit is outside, on a rustic wooden seat, in the shade.

**SIN NAM HUAT
ROASTED CHICKEN
AND DUCK RICE**
59 Lebuh Cintra,
George Town
9am-5pm, daily
Part of a franchise, this place in the middle of town is spick and span and the young guys who work here always have big, welcoming grins. You order off a tablet; the roasted chicken is awesome and you can choose either plain or oiled rice. The chai boey soup, deliciously puckery with plenty of preserved mustard leaf, is terrific.

**KIM POH ROAST
CHICKEN AND DUCK
RICE**
334 Lintang Slim, Taman Desa Green
8am-10pm, daily
Large, clean and orderly, this place is nirvana for the poultry fiend. Roast duck is a hot seller and it's rich with smoky, soy flavours. There's an exemplary poached chicken and the indecisive can order a mix of meats. All the way up to a combo of roast pork, duck, chicken and char siew (BBQ pork).

**JIT SENG HONG KONG
ROAST DUCK RICE**
246 Lebuh Carnarvon,
George Town
12pm-3pm (approx), daily
Under the fabulously decrepit Star Hotel, folk wait patiently for 12pm, when Mr Lam turns up with a scooterful of his celebrated duck. Then, it's all on for young and old – they only pause for breath when the meats (there's roast pork and BBQ pork too) run out. It's three to four hours, every day, of non-stop chopping. You get a special bean sauce with your juicy bird here – delicious.

**GOH THEW CHIK
HAINAN CHICKEN RICE**
338 Lebuh Chulia,
George Town
11am-6pm, Thursday-Tuesday, 11am-3pm, Wednesday
The text-book Hainan chicken comes doused in soy sauce and the flavoursome rice is wonderful, even on its own. Although in the thick of the tourist hub, plenty of locals pack this place every day; it's been in business for decades (the original Mr Goh Thew Chik came from Hainan Island more than 70 years ago). They also do a stunning roast chicken.

**HOT BOWL NYONYA
DELIGHTS**
58C Jalan Rangoon,
George Town
8am-3pm (closed Monday)
Most famous for white curry mee (curry mee with the spice paste served on the side) but the boneless poached chicken rice is superb; some say the best in town. Tender and juicy, it strikes all the right soft, sweet and savoury chords. Plus, it's an air-conned haven.

**WEN CHANG HAINAN
CHICKEN RICE**
63 Lebuh Cintra,
George Town
10.30am-7.30pm, daily
The current owner's parents started the business in 1967 and although the address is not the original, the recipe and methods surely are. The coffee shop ambience is basic and there's no menu as such – everyone knows to order either the roast or poached bird, with their killer homemade garlic-chilli sauce, fragrant rice and drizzled with delicious, soy-sauce laden juices.

Something Fishy

Ringed by ocean and with a thriving fishing industry, it's logical that there's good seafood in Penang. Fish restaurants are casual – a bit ramshackle even. Some are on the beach with no walls as such; you can literally smell the briny air and watch fishermen puttering about in boats.

JUST-COOKED POMFRET AND SQUID AT BEACH CORNER

FISH AND SEAFOOD PLUCKED LIVE FROM TANKS is the ultimate in fresh eating and lots of places offer this. Critters are charged by the weight and prices will vary, depending on the season. They tend to be cooked whole for the best flavour; cooked lobsters, clams, prawns, crabs and the like need to be wrested from shells at the table, and fin fish come complete with heads and a full set of bones. So be prepared for that. Whatever is on the menu, cooking techniques are kept simple, to highlight taste and texture. Penangites don't mess around too much with their seafood; uncomplicated is best.

Steaming: good for varieties such as sea bass, red snapper, thread fin and white pomfret. Typical styles include Teochew, using punchy ingredients like sour plums, salted vegetables and ginger, tempered with tofu and tomato. Or Nyonya, where spices and feisty aromatics such as chilli, turmeric, *belacan* and lemongrass are common. Then there's Thai-style (you're near the border, after all), featuring kaffir lime leaves, chilli, galangal, lemongrass and ginger flower. Classic, simple Chinese flavourings (soy sauce, ginger, garlic and green onion) are standard offerings too.

Grilling: charcoal fire is better than gas, for smoky richness. Slightly oily fish like mackerel or stingray are best for grilling as they have sturdier flesh that stands up well to the direct heat. Served with sauces for dipping; tamarind with chilli, or straight chilli paste are usual.

Frying: fleshy white fish such as grouper, black pomfret and versatile red snapper are suited to deep-frying; they're fried whole, either plain, marinated first in spices or soy or slathered with a spiced-up sambal-like paste.

Crabs: crabs should feel heavy for their size. They're expensive so when choosing, ensure all legs are intact and that shells are not cracked. Whole charcoal-baked crabs, crab stir-fried with noodles, and fried sweet and sour crabs, in plenty of gooey sauce, are popular. *Kam heong* crab, where crab is stir-fried with a heady mix of curry leaves, dried shrimp garlic, oyster and soy sauces, is a favourite. Some restaurants present baked crab with pickles and dipping sauces while others serve it plain, to best savour the sweet flesh. Either way, prepare for some mess as you eat.

Prawns: you'll encounter a few different species – king, tiger and mantis for example. Fresh prawns should have no discolouration and should smell sweetly of the sea. There's a fresh water prawn called *udang galah* which has succulent flesh and a head stuffed with tomalley (a.k.a. goo); locals love to suck this out. Prawns are grilled, steamed or stir-fried; sambal, black pepper and curry are favourite flavourings. 'Nestum', a brand of packaged cereal food, is often used as a deep-fry coating, as is batter. Mantis prawns are particularly sweet and ▷

meaty and are often steamed with just a little garlic and ginger. Or deep-fried. Freshwater prawns take well to steaming – often with egg white, ginger and rice wine – as well as to simmering in a punchy spice and curry leaf gravy. *Assam* prawns are those cooked in their shells with a thick tamarind, sugar and dark soy coating sauce.

Clams and Oysters: clams are popular Chinese-style, where they're steamed or stir-fried with flavours such as garlic, chilli, coriander, ginger or rice wine. A zingy sambal-like paste is also popular. Slim, long bamboo (razor) clams are juicy, with a chewy texture, and are good stir-fried with black beans, ginger, garlic and spring onions. Or just steamed. *Kappa mee suah* is a dish of clams cooked with noodles, in an egg-enriched sauce. Oysters are either steamed or baked, topped with combinations of black beans, chilli, garlic, ginger and soy. You'll see them baked with cheese and cooked in an omelette, too.

Squid: small squid are flash-boiled or fried whole, and served with simple embellishments such as garlic oil or soy and ginger. Larger ones are stir-fried, in slices, with ginger, garlic chives and soy sauce, or lightly coated with batter or salted egg yolk, deep-fried, and served with different dipping sauces.❖

Stir-fried squid at Da Shu Xia

Umbrellas near Beach Corner

FRESH FISH
GRILLED • STEAMED • DEEP FRIED
SWEET • SOUR • 3 FLAVOURS • CHILLI

Rainbow lobster at Bali Hai

Prawn noodles, Sunshine Bay

Setting up at Bali Hai

COAL-BAKED PRAWNS
AND CRABS AT SEA
PEARL LAGOON CAFE

WHERE TO EAT

BALI HAI SEAFOOD MARKET
90 Persiaran Gurney, George Town
6.30am-2.30pm, 5pm-10.30pm, daily

Mantis prawns? Check. Tiger prawns? Check. Rock cod? Sea bass? Lobster and oysters? Check, check and keep checking. If it swims, chances are, they've got it. They even have the hard-to-get *empurau* from Sarawak, Malaysia's most expensive fish. Its unique, sweet flavour is said to come from eating wild fruit that drops off trees into their river habitats.

PANG HAINAN SEAFOOD
501 K&L, Jalan Tanjung Bungah, Tanjung Tokong
12pm-2.30pm, 6pm-10.30pm (closed Monday)

A way up the coast but, joy of joys, they're open for lunch (not all seafood places are). The comprehensive menu has every fishy whim covered, from mantis prawns, crab, scallops, oysters, plenty of fin fish, squid and clams, to rice paddy frogs.

SEA PEARL LAGOON CAFE
338 Mukim 18, Jalan Tokong Thai Pak Koong
11am-9.30pm (closed alternate Wednesdays)

No one seems to know how long they've been around; some say "since the 1920s" and others, "forever". The location is fabulous, right on the beach and next to the atmospheric Tua Pek Kong temple. Simple and basic, the menu is all about coal-baked prawns and crabs. You order these by the 500-gram portion and eat off plastic plates, using your hands, forks and a wooden roller to crack the shells open.

DA SHU XIA
177 Lebuh Victoria, George Town
11am-10pm, daily

Smack in the historic core of George Town, this is handy if you're staying close and want to walk to dinner. It's always crowded with happy groups. Choose your seafood from iced tray displays and tell the staff how you want it cooked. If you're not really sure, no worries; they'll offer options that best suit your selection.

OCEAN GREEN RESTAURANT
Jalan Sultan Ahmad Shah, George Town
12pm-3pm, 6pm-10.30pm, daily

With a stunning, seaside location, this is a favourite for wedding parties; do check out the time-warped Paramount Hotel right behind (see pg 72), and the lovely beach out the front. Steamed tiger prawns with house-made chilli sauce is a winner of a dish and their steamed fish in curry sauce, with okra, tomato and mint leaves, is also delicious.

SOMETHING FISHY

BEACH CORNER SEAFOOD RESTAURANT
72D Jalan Batu Ferringhi, Batu Ferringhi
12pm-2.30pm, 6pm-10pm (closed Wednesday)

Locals clamour for the deep-fried *popiah*, bursting with vegetables, marinated pork and prawn. There are all the seafood standards – steamed fish, baked crabs, prawns with noodles in *tom yum* gravy and *kam heong* squid. It's relaxed, is right on the beach and is fairly quiet during the day.

SUNSHINE BAY
569B Jalan Tanjung Bungah, Tanjung Bungah
5pm-10.30pm (closed Tuesday)

The seafood noodle dishes are gorgeous, with their tasty, thick sauces, sweet nuggets of crab, lobster or prawn and comforting, noodley chew. Steamed stingray with lime, chilli, garlic and ginger is worth ordering too.

DE HAPPY
58 Jalan Macalister, George Town
11am-12am, daily

It's halal here so no chance of a cheeky chardonnay with your fish. But people flock for the local flavours worked around seafood plucked from tanks – go the claypot fish with yam route, or whole fish, marinated in spices, Nyonya-style, then deep-fried. Or live mantis prawns – delish. It's close to the centre of town and, hooray, open for lunch.

Sometimes, even avowed Spice Cadets need a break from chilli and complex flavours. All that heat can be exhausting! Here's some soup noodle action that's gentle, soothing and subtle, for when your taste buds want to notch it down a gear or three.

KOAY TEOW TH'NG

Koay teow th'ng lives in the shadows of its more famous noodle dish cousins; many visitors to Penang have never heard of it before arriving. It's easy to dismiss as it's pale and unfussy, consisting of fresh rice noodles (the same ones used for *char koay teow*), a delicious clear soup ('*th'ng*' is 'soup' in Hokkien) and various garnishes. Fish balls, boiled meats and a few bits of mustard leaf, choi sum or other green vegetable are the usual. The secret to its sweet tastiness is the addition of garlic that's been deep-fried in lard until golden, then slicked onto the soup just before serving. The seductive nuttiness you can smell as your bowl is set in front of you is that garlic. Good versions of *koay teow th'ng* use homemade fish balls that have plenty of springy bite and fulsome flavour. Different stalls offer different garnishes – duck meat is popular, as is chicken. Minced pork, pork intestines, wontons and cubes of coagulated ▷

KOAY TEOW TH'NG

pork blood are other possibilities.

The clear stock is made from pork, chicken or duck bones, or combinations thereof. It should be savoury with a faint sweetness and taste of its main, meaty ingredients; noodles should be ultra fresh and silky smooth. The finished soup is served with a dish of chopped chillies, to combine with soy sauce at the table as a dip for garnishes, and *sambal* to heat things up if you want. The perfect dish for breakfast, especially if you've eaten too much the day before, *koay teow th'ng* is very popular with locals and you'll see versions of it all over the place, throughout the day and evening.❖

Pitt Street Koay Teow Th'ng's fish balls

113 Duck Meat Koay Teow Soup

Pitt Street Koay Teow Th'ng

94

WHERE TO EAT

113 DUCK MEAT KOAY TEOW SOUP

113 Lebuh Melayu, George Town
6.30am-12pm (closed Sunday)

They tend to run out of their signature duck soup noodles early; this is one of the most popular KTT outlets in town. You can have duck intestines, duck gizzards and other duck spare parts in your soup, or soy sauce-cooked tofu, egg, pig intestines or chicken's feet on the side. Or just more duck meat. Not that the dish runs short on protein – they pile fish and pork balls in, and both are homemade and delicious.

7 VILLAGE NOODLE HOUSE

37 Lorong Abu Siti, George Town
8am-9pm, daily

Like many established businesses in Penang, this one started as a roadside stall (in Butterworth) decades ago; today there are multiple branches here and across the mainland. On the menu, KTT is called by its Mandarin name, *guo tiao tang*, but the accompanying pictures will allay any confusion. As they've been making this since 1956, it goes without saying they've perfected the dish and also do a wonderful dry version, doused in soy sauce.

LUM LAI DUCK MEAT KOAY TEOW TH'NG

Cecil Street Market, 40-48 Lebuh Cecil, George Town
7.30am-7pm (closed alternate Wednesdays)

This place is in the Cecil Street Market, where there are other street-food gems too, including *pasembur*, *Hokkien* mee and curry mee. The duck-laden stock in the KTT has sweet, porky undertones and the noodles are generously topped with duck meat slices, cubes of congealed duck blood, fish balls and fish cakes.

PITT STREET KOAY TEOW TH'NG

183 Lebuh Carnarvon, George Town
8am-4pm, Tuesday-Saturday, 8am-1pm, Sunday

All roads to The Ultimate KTT lead here. They hand-make their fish balls daily using eel meat; they're wonderfully bouncy and full-flavoured. Anything else in the soup (duck, pork intestines, fresh noodles, lettuce and pork 'fillet', made from minced meat) plays mere second fiddle to those wondrous balls (you get three), although the lard-fried garlic is pretty scrumptious. They offer a dry version of KTT too but just about everyone has the eel ball soup version. The name comes from the shop's former location, if you're wondering.

KOAY TEOW TH'NG STALL @ CLARKE STREET

Lebuh Clarke, near Jalan Argyll, George Town
7am-2pm (closed Tuesday)

The robust chicken stock (they boil whole, old birds for hours), the selection of four different types of balls (plain fish, fried fish, pork and pork-ginger) and the choice of noodles (you can have yellow or rice vermicelli as well as the usual fresh rice) have made this second generation-run place a go-to for locals for more than 30 years. It's tucked down an alley off Lebuh Clarke, but not at all tricky to find. Order a side of poached chicken with liver and heart or try their dry version of the dish, which is sauced with a sweetish, hearty mixture of stock, soy sauces and sesame oil.

KEDAI KOPI SOON YUEN

25-27 Jalan Kuala Kangsar, George Town
7am-11.30am, daily

An old-school *kopi tiam* in the thick of George Town, known for its duck-based KTT broth and especially tasty homemade fish balls. Order a side plate of sliced duck meat to truly gild the lily. It gets frantic here on account of its being smack in the middle of a busy street food market, which is well worth a look see.

BEACHSIDE BARS

Languid breezes, lapping waves, swaying palms and that promising sound of a cocktail shaker doing its cocktail thing: a beachside bar is what you want when you're dodging Real Life for a week or two. And Penang has a few places to indulge this ultimate escapist fantasy, gin and tonic firmly in hand.

VIEW FROM THE
BAR AT THE
RASA SAYANG

AT THE RASA
SAYANG RESORT,
BATU FERRINGHI

BEACHSIDE BARS

BEACH BLANKET BABYLON
32 Jalan Sultan Ahmad Shah
George Town
11am-12am, daily

A little scruffy around the edges, this local fav looks best at night under clever lighting, but then again, don't we all. Come during the day anyway as the setting is sublime and it's quiet then. Set into an old mansion, the outdoor bar faces the sea, with a few tables and chairs that are so near The Drink (ocean), you're nearly in it. They've a decent wine list, make a good cocktail and have a very long happy hour, from 11am-8pm, daily.

POOL BAR
Golden Sands by Shangri La
Batu Ferringhi
11am-11.45pm, daily

Admire the sweeping, 1970s architecture of this stalwart four star, then pick your way through the families cavorting poolside to the bar near the beach. Happy hour runs from 5pm-8pm daily, when a selection of beers, wines and mixed drinks are half price. Plan this one for a trip up the coast to Batu Ferringhi; it's not exactly close to George Town. About 30 minutes in a taxi will get you there.

FARQUHAR'S BAR
Eastern & Oriental Hotel
10 Lebuh Farquhar,
George Town
11am-12am, daily

The outdoors part is more poolside than beachside although you are technically next to the coast. Let's not quibble over technicalities. Let's also not take issue with the fact that come lunch time, they serve a roast beef and Yorkshire pudding-centric buffet inside because there are no words for this scenario in the tropics but hey, each to their own. *Your own should*

Three Sixty Rooftop Bar

Drinks at the Golden S

Golden Sands Shangri La

Three Sixty Rooftop Bar

Beach Blanket Babylon

be a cocktail in the warm air; resist the temptation of the interior air-con so you can take in the grand exterior of one of Asia's loveliest old hostelries.

THREE SIXTY ROOFTOP BAR
25 Lebuh Farquhar, George Town
4pm-2am, daily

It's the highest bar in George Town and the views from here, over both the city and the Straits, are spectacular. There's no other vantage point like it and, while you're not precisely by the beach, you're hovering right above it.

PINANG RESTAURANT AND BAR
Rasa Sayang Resort, Batu Ferringhi
10am-10pm, daily

Another resort that's been around for decades, this one overlooks an especially beautiful stretch of the beach at Batu Ferringhi. It's idyllic; come for sunset when they sound a gong to mark the start of happy hour (5.30pm-7.30pm). The bar runs from a cute wooden cabana, and decking for tables goes right to the beachfront edge of the property. Staff here are particularly friendly and helpful.

THE BUNGALOW
Lone Pine, 97 Jalan Batu Ferringi,
11am-11pm, daily

Not really a bar as such but there's no issue at all with taking a table on the terrace and zoning out over a beer or cocktail. The beach is just over THERE so come in the arvo and wait for the sunset when the vibe is mellow. Inside is the smart-casual Batubar (open 10am-1am), with a tapas menu, cocktails and wine list. The property centres around the original old bungalow, converted to a small hotel in 1948 and now boutique digs with 90 rooms. ❖

Singapore Sling, Beach Blanket Babylon

Three Sixty Rooftop Bar

Peranakan Penang

'Peranakan' is the name given to the Fujian Chinese whose forebears intermarried with local Malays. They spawned a unique culture that's a colourful mix of Chinese and Malay; historically this manifested in their dress, architecture, crafts and cuisine.

A BEAUTIFUL ROOM
AT THE PINANG
PERANAKAN MANSION

PENGAT AT
THE LEGEND
NYONYA HOUSE

Nasi ulam being prepared

Chicken curry kapitan,
The Legend Nyonya House

The Peranakans came from the business class and were considered somewhat elite. Many were British educated and fluent in several languages including English; they were known as the 'King's Chinese' for their loyalty to the British crown. They're also referred to as the Straits Chinese, because the main settlements were in Singapore, Penang and Malacca, all in the Straits of Malacca. You'll also hear them called 'Baba Nyonyas'. The Babas are the men and the Nyonyas the women, and the cuisine is commonly referred to as 'Nyonya' cooking.

Nyonya food is an example of true, fusion cooking. It's highly refined and time consuming to prepare; culinary skills were prized and it was unthinkable for a prospective Nyonya bride to not be an excellent cook. A blending of Chinese ingredients and styles with Malay spices and cooking techniques gave rise to unique interpretations of dishes that are at once tangy, aromatic, spicy and herbal. Fragrant dishes like *assam* (tamarind) fish, beef *rendang, jeu hoo char* (a mix of finely shredded carrot, onion, mushroom, pork and cuttlefish eaten in lettuce leaves as a hand-held wrap) and curry *kapitan*, a rich, thick curry redolent of galangal, lemongrass and kaffir lime leaves, are typical. *Pie tee* and *assam laksa* had their origins with the Nyonyas.

Nyonya dishes rely on the painstaking grinding of fresh spices and herbs for their punch and texture. Pastes for flavouring curry, sambals and dressings are pounded fresh, using a mortar and pestle. Vegetables are finely shredded using a knife or cleaver and fresh coconut flesh is grated by hand. This cooking is laborious and recipes tend not to be written down. Each household guarded their kitchen secrets closely; measuring was done using a system called *'agak agak'* or 'most likely/probably'. This cooking by 'feel' and experience is still practised by the keepers of authentic Nyonya food ways in Penang; luckily, there are a handful of dedicated restaurants where you can go to try this food. The best ones are family run, using recipes passed down from previous generations.

NYONYA DISHES INCLUDE:
Nasi kunyit – A Malay dish of turmeric-flavoured yellow glutinous rice, associated with celebrations for a one-month old baby. Often served with a meat curry (chicken is common), which in turn has origins in Indian-Malay fusion cooking. Flavours for the curry include Indian seed spices (cardamom, coriander, cumin, fennel), lemongrass and kaffir lime leaves. ▷

PERANAKAN PENANG

Pengat – A traditional Malay sweet dish comprising coconut milk, palm sugar, various fruits and cubes of boiled root vegetables, like taro. The Nyonyas served it on the fifteenth day of the Lunar New Year. It's similar to *bubur cha cha*.

Nasi ulam – A dish of cold rice mixed with various fresh, fine cut herbs and spices, including ginger flower, turmeric, betel leaves, penny wort leaves, lemongrass and kaffir lime, all painstakingly sliced incredibly finely. Toasted coconut, shallots, dried shrimp and toasted *belacan* are also added.

Bak chang – A rice dumpling similar to Southern Chinese *zhongzi*, with a spiced filling of minced pork with candied winter melon and ground roasted peanuts. Pea flower dyes the rice blue, and pandan leaves are sometimes used as the wrapping instead of the usual bamboo leaves.

Kerabu bee hoon – A salad of rice vermicelli, *sambal belacan*, lime juice and finely chopped herbs and spices. Other salad dishes (*kerabu* denotes 'salad') include *kerabu bok nee* (cloud ear fungus), *kerabu kay* (chicken), *kerabu kay khar* (chicken feet), *kerabu timun* (cucumber), *kerabu kobis* (cabbage), *kerabu kacang botol* (wing bean) and *kerabu bak poey* (pork skin).

Enche kabin – Chicken marinated in coconut and spice paste then deep-fried until the skin is golden and crisp. Mmmmmm.

Pie tee – A fine, crisp pastry tart shell filled with a spicy, sweet mixture of thinly sliced vegetables and prawns.

Otak otak – A mousse-like spiced fish paste wrapped in banana leaves then grilled or steamed. There are versions of this dish all over South-East Asia but the Nyonya one contains a herb called *duan kaduk or* 'wild pepper leaf'.

PINANG PERANAKAN MANSION
29 Lebuh Church, George Town
9.30am-5pm, daily

Housed in a stately old green mansion with strong elements of Peranakan design, this amazing museum is the perfect place to understand a little about this singular culture. It's been lavishly refurbished to showcase how the upper Baba-Nyonya echelons lived, with extensive displays of antiques, artefacts, clothing and furniture. The family rooms are fascinating, and include a traditional bridal room complete with an ornate bed festooned with incredible hand-embroidered details. The collection of Nyonya jewellery, that fills an entire room, is astounding. The huge kitchen, filled to the brim with cooking accoutrements, demonstrates just how important food preparation was in these households. ❖

Nyonya portrait at the Pinang Peranakan Mansion

Chicken kerabu

Spread of dishes at Little Kitchen

Exterior of the Pinang Peranakan Mansion

Perut Rumah Nyonya

Wing bean *kerabu*

Bak chang

WHERE TO EAT

KEBAYA
14A Lorong Stewart,
George Town
6pm-8pm, daily
Arguably the nicest dining room in all of George Town is part of the boutique Seven Terraces hotel. The chef adds his own fine-dining refinements to Nyonya dishes; *otak otak*, for example, is cooked in pastry, rather than the usual banana leaf, and *onde onde* are served in a warm, coconut milk soup.

LITTLE KITCHEN
179 Lebuh Noordin,
George Town
6.30pm-8.30pm,
Monday-Friday
Baba Jay's little restaurant is chock full of family memorabilia and trinkets; this is his ancestral home. Order the *nasi ulam*, which Baba Jay prepares at the table complete with an entertaining commentary on all the fresh herbs.

NYONYA BABA CUISINE
44 Jalan Nagor,
George Town
11am-2.30pm, 6pm-9.30pm (closed Tuesday)
Established in 1976, this place is a gem, with a distinctly nostalgic feel. The current owner, Khoo Siew Eng, took over from her aunt and does the bulk of the cooking from recipes that were handed down from her grandmother.

PERANAKAN PENANG

PERUT RUMAH NYONYA
4-8 Jalan Bawasah,
George Town
11am-3pm, 6pm-10pm, daily
The old bungalow is lovely, the service is friendly and the food, pretty darned great. You'll find plenty on the extensive menu to entice; black vinegar pork, *otak otak*, *jeu hoo char*, *assam* prawns and spring roll-like fried *popiah*.

AUNTIE GAIK LEAN'S
1 Lebuh Bishop,
George Town
12pm-2pm, 6pm-9.30pm (closed Monday)
The menu is a greatest hits line-up of Nyonya favourites – the restaurant itself, right in central George Town, is hugely popular. It's hard to single out particular dishes as it's all good. But the specialities of *nasi ulam* and *kerabu bee hoon* are tops. As is the *nasi kunyit*, with fragrant chicken curry.

THE LEGEND NYONYA HOUSE
2 Gat Lebuh Chulia,
George Town
11am-10pm, daily
Handy to the thick of the George Town action and with a stylish, yet family-friendly vibe, this newish place does a cracking chicken *kapitan* and lush *pengat*. They run daily specials, offer good value sets for lunch and present everything ever so prettily on traditional china.

CUTTLEFISH AND *KANG KONG* FOR *LOK LOK*, AT PADANG BROWN HAWKER CENTRE

Steamboat … and *lok lok*. It's hard to separate the two (so we haven't), as the underlying principle – cooking small bits of food by immersing them in simmering liquid then eating them dipped in sauce – is same-same. But different. Here's how.

STEAMBOAT

Lok lok means 'dip dip' and it's a hawker dish that's perfect for groups or solo diners, whereas steamboat is served at specialty restaurants and works best as a collective eating activity. With *lok lok*, the cooking medium is water and the various items you dip in it are on wooden skewers which are colour coded to denote price. Items range from fish balls, meats, seafood, vegetables, tofu, quail eggs and dumplings to crab sticks; once heated in the water and drained, there are rich dipping sauces (like satay, dried shrimp and chilli), to douse the morsels in. Some hawker centres have tables set up with a pot of boiling water and plates of skewered bits ready to go; you share a spot with other *lok lok*-ers and hoe into whatever takes your fancy. The vendor will tote up the damage based on your empty sticks. There are mobile *lok lok* carts too which mainly appear at night. The best vendors make their own sauces ▷

SETTING UP A TABLE AT CHIOW LIN STEAMBOAT RESTAURANT

At Goh Huat Seng

Dipping *lok lok* in boiling water

Selection of sticks, Padang Brown

Items for steamboat at De'Luck

STEAMBOAT

and it's quite ok to mix these to your taste; note that the cooking liquid is not meant to be consumed. Unlike steamboat, where it absolutely is.

Steamboat is fun to eat and there are many different styles, determined largely by the flavour of the stock. Some stocks are based on pork bones, others on fish head; Thai *tom yum* and *assam laksa* broths are becoming trendy. It's thought steamboat originated in Mongolia, spread through China and then found its way to parts of Asia. In Malaysia it used to be reserved for special occasions but these days, it's very common.

You either order your bits from a menu, or there'll be a buffet-style arrangement where you choose what you fancy. You get a small gas-fired (or electric induction) element on your table for the broth – some places still use charcoal-burning copper hotpots, with funnel-shaped 'chimneys' and a circular trough of bubbling stock. You simply dunk your selected bits in the stock, let them simmer away then retrieve them to your bowl using a slotted ladle. Once everything's been cooked in it, the broth tastes even better. ✤

Goh Huat Seng

Goh Huat Seng

112

WHERE TO EAT

GOH HUAT SENG
59A Lebuh Kimberley,
George Town
5pm-9.30pm (closed
Tuesday)
One of the oldest Teochew restaurants in George Town, with an original interior and old copper, charcoal-burning steamboat pots. You choose set dishes from a board, from two plates all the way up to 12. Broth comes already loaded with cabbage and beancurd and the sides include prawns, noodles, fish balls, wan tan, and soft, egg tofu.

DE'LUCK LAKSA STEAMBOAT
17 Jalan Zainal Abidin,
George Town
5.30pm-1am (closed
Monday)
Combine an assam laksa fix with a steamboat one – win win. This low-key restaurant is off the usual tourist tracks, attracting (mainly) younger locals who love the novel, unorthodox approach to steamboat. Choose your bits from the fridge while the friendly owner, David, cranks the heat under your pot of laksa broth.

TOWN STEAMBOAT RESTAURANT
63 Jalan Macalister,
George Town
5pm-12am, daily
With a huge buffet selection for your hotpot and very reasonable prices, this barn-like restaurant is busy and congenial. Choose broths (you can have two) then pile everything in – the seafood selection is decent. There are more than 10 sauces, free-flow soft drinks, plenty of desserts (including ice-cream) and meats to barbecue, in butter, at your table too.

HUO TAN WANG CHARCOAL STEAMBOAT
6 Jalan Nagor,
George Town
5.30pm-12am (closed
Monday)
The delicious, milky stock is made by boiling dried squid, fresh chicken and pork bones for eight hours – it's lip smacking. Everything from fish to pork to mushrooms tastes wonderful simmered in its delicious goodness and – bonus – they fuel their steamboats with charcoal.

YI BING QING FISH HEAD STEAMBOAT
16 Jalan Nagor,
George Town
6pm-1am, daily
Another traditional-style place in a cosy shophouse, the menu is simple – choose fish head or fish fillet steamboat and either a sour-spicy or non-spicy broth. Everything is super fresh, the stock is hefty and the basic fish head set has chunks of deep-fried head, pork meat balls, cabbage, yam and seaweed. Order a side of deep-fried fish skin and come early as it gets packed.

STEAMBOAT
CHIOW LIN STEAMBOAT
30 Lorong Abu Siti,
George Town
5pm-5am, daily
Chongqing-style steamboat is their thing and they offer a dual pot system, meaning you can choose two broths. Herbal Tonic Soup is popular and, for the brave, so is Dry Pot Frog which, despite the name, is a tongue-burning soup, and not 'dry' at all. But it is froggy.

PADANG BROWN HAWKER CENTRE
Between Jalan Anson and Jalan Perak, George Town
2pm-7pm (closed Thursday)
There are plenty of lok lok stands around but if you want to go 'Full Immersion Local', head here in the late afternoon and join the dipping fray. Take a seat at one of the set-up tables, help yourself to the homemade sauce selection (mix them to taste) and dip yourself crazy. Great fun.

PULAU TIKUS MARKET HAWKER CENTRE
Jalan Pasar,
George Town
6pm-12pm (closed Wednesday)
Choose from around 30 items and six sauces, including a delicious satay, and mayonnaise with ginger flower. Like many lok lok outlets, items are mainly processed (meat and fish balls, crab sticks etc) but there's raw seafood and fresh meat offerings as well.

THE BIG STINK

Skunky, spiky and pretty darned kooky, it's hard to be ho-hum about durian. With its soft, buttery flesh, voluptuous flavours and unique, cloying smell (which some dramatically liken to an open sewer or fermenting, unwashed socks), durian is something you either love … or don't love. Yes, it really does reek. That pong can literally blanket a room and dominate it for days; for this reason, durian isn't allowed in hotels, hospitals or on public transport.

THE FAMOUS
DURIAN ICE-CREAM
AT KEK SENG
COFFEE SHOP

THE BIG STINK

Durians are huge – depending on the variety (there are more than 100 in Malaysia and even more cultivars), a single one weighs from one to four kilograms. The thorny skin is thick and green-brownish, and the lobes of flesh are prised from five interior 'compartments'. Flesh colour varies from pale yellow through to orangey-red and it can be consumed at various stages of ripeness. Determining ripeness and opening a durian both require experience, skill and thick gloves. The word 'durian' comes from a Malay word for 'spike' and that menacing exterior can do damage.

Durians are a big deal in Penang, which claims to produce the finest in the world. The main season runs from May to July (depending on weather), when there's a frenzy of eating and mega bucks dropped – durians fetch in the hundreds of ringgit each. You'll see (and smell) vendors' carts dotted about the island but there's a concentration up Jalan Macalister. (Set off on foot from the junction of Macalister and Jalan Penang and you'll come to some within a few blocks.) Even if you don't intend to indulge (coward!), it's fascinating to watch the selecting, weighing, opening, purchasing and consuming activity. It's serious business. Locals will only buy from reputable dealers as crooked practices do exist. Such as spraying under-ripe or sub-par fruits with durian-scented water, to enhance their aroma. ▷

POPULAR TYPES OF DURIAN

Different varieties have different characteristics – the colour, texture, aroma and flavour can all subtly vary. Here are just a few types you'll encounter in Penang.

RED PRAWN
(also called *ang he* and *udang merah*).
Reddish-orangey flesh that's sweet-tasting and complex in flavour. In Penang, this is one of the most sought-after varieties. The skin has short spikes.

MUSANG KING
One of the most popular types currently, the yellowish flesh is particularly creamy and has a slightly bitter edge.

D24
Very thick, mouth-filling flesh with a milder flavour and less of a smell. The flavour is neutral in the sweet/bitter stakes, making it a good choice for the durian beginner.

BLACK THORN
(also called *orchee* and *duri hitam*).
The flesh has a bright orange hue, is very creamy and mild-flavoured. It's not so sweet, with a slightly bitter finish. Very fleshy despite abundant seeds.

SUSU
(milk durian).
Very pale flesh with little fibre and sweet/bitter milky flavours. Incredibly creamy.

HOR LOR
(also called *labu*).
'Hor Lor' means 'gourd' and this best describes the slightly hourglass shape. With small seeds and yellow flesh, this durian is sweet and not too complex in flavour.

Kek Seng interior

Durian flesh ready to buy

Durian cake at Passion Heart Cafe

Durian *bubur cha cha* at My Armenian Cafe

A sign for durian on Jalan Macalister

Did you know…?

+ Durian is chock-full of vitamins and minerals, including B-complex vitamins (unusual for a fruit), vitamins C and E, potassium, zinc, iron and magnesium.

+ Durian is high in carbohydrates; 100 grams delivers 21% of daily carb requirements.

+ Despite its custardy opulence, durian contains no cholesterol and is actually good for those wanting to reduce their own. As that same custardy opulence might suggest, durian is full of monounsaturated fats (the flesh is around 7% fat) which can be beneficial in preventing cardiovascular diseases.

+ Durian is rich in a substance called tryptophan which the body converts to serotonin. Serotonin helps you sleep well, and feel generally relaxed and happy. Durian is also said to improve libido although the dreaded 'durian breath' you get after eating it could well knock your significant other's urges right on the head.

+ A durian falling off a tree can kill on account of its weight and sharp, jagged exterior, and several people do die this way each year. Ripe fruits must be allowed to fall from the tree, ideally, they shouldn't be cut off. To prevent injury to both people and fruit, nets are positioned under branches to catch ripe durians as they fall.

+ The weight of the edible pulp of the fruit is only 15-30% of its total mass, depending on the type.

+ Durians are highly perishable. They ripen within two to four days after falling off the tree and lose eating quality after about five days. Once opened, the flesh should be eaten within a day.

+ There's a common belief that terrible things happen to a person who drinks alcohol and eats durian on the same day but science doesn't fully support this. The combo will maybe not make you feel so great, in any case.

WHERE TO EAT DURIAN

TNG SIANG HOCK TRADING
74 Jalan Dr Lim Chwee Leong, George Town
11 am-11 pm, Monday-Saturday
An indoor venue that's one of the few places offering durian year-round, regardless of the Penang season. They source from all over Malaysia and during the local harvest, have an all-you-can-eat durian buffet. Yes, really. If you're too chicken to try the real deal, or are't here for the season (damn!), try a durian-flavoured dessert; read on. Pulp freezes well for pancakes, cakes, ice-cream and pastries and many places make sweet durian treats, year round.

WHERE TO EAT DURIAN DESSERTS

PASSION HEART CAFE
83 Jalan Muntri, George Town
12pm-10.30pm, Monday, Wednesday-Saturday, 12pm-9pm, Sunday
Owner Nely Koon is famous for her wonderful baking. Her cafe offers some 20-odd cakes including coffee meringue cake and a Black Forest tizzed up with red wine. It's great stuff. One of the best sellers is *cempedak* cake, made using the fresh fruit when it's in season. A relative of jackfruit, the *cempedak* is highly fragrant. Then there's Nely's durian cake, also a stunner. It may look simple and rustic but each mouthful is loaded with delicious durian flavour and scent.

KEK SENG COFFEE SHOP
382-384 Jalan Penang, George Town
8.30am-5.30pm, daily
They're famous for their homemade durian ice-cream, which you can enjoy solo or as a topping for their (also legendary) *ice kacang* (see pg 120). The 1906 shophouse interior has a wonderfully old-time feel; check out the wooden bench seating and fabulous tiles. The current owner doesn't know exactly when they started with the durian ice-cream but says her grandfather-in-law was offering it here back in the 1950s.

DURIAN HAVEN
16 Lebuh Armenian, George Town
1 am-7.30pm, daily
Durian cendol, durian mochi, durian cheesecake, durian coffee, musang king biscuits; the durian-centric menu at this newish, modern cafe makes it crystal clear why you're here. Durian newbies will love the sweet, subtle notes of fruit in the intricately stacked crepe cake and ganache-topped

cheesecake, while hard-core devotees should go for the creamy durian puffs – just biting into one releases those unmistakable, durian-laden vapours.

MEN'S KITCHEN
71 Lebuh Armenian, George Town
9.30am-6.30pm, daily
Durian Portuguese tarts are what they are known for although their 'ice fire roll', a deep-fried roll of durian flesh in a fine, crisp, flaky shell, and the baked durian buns are rather stupendous too. Those tarts though. They have a filling that's rich and thick with durian-ness and you won't find their like anywhere else. They also charge up the flamer to finish off a durian brûlée, fry durian wan tan and spring rolls and even sell durian-flavoured *kaya* (egg jam).

MY ARMENIAN CAFE
98 Lebuh Armenian, George Town
10am-8pm, daily
Although the menu here is broader than either durian or even desserts, they're nuts about the smelly stuff. Durian pancakes, durian cheesecake and durian *bubur cha cha* are all superb and, even better, they've a shop next door filled with packaged durian goodies – freeze-dried durian, durian lollies and durian-filled chocolates – to take home. The sister-owners are charming and friendly.

ICE KACANG AT
LOKE THYE KEE

Nothing says 'the tropics' like a bowl of *ice kacang*. And if you reckon a tower of shaved ice slathered in creamed corn, red beans, grass jelly, syrup, evaporated milk and chunks of agar-agar is weird, you need to let it go. It's perfection; trust us.

ICE KACANG

Ice kacang (pronounced 'ka-chang') literally means 'bean ice' as it originally comprised red beans and ice. It had a precursor too in the ice balls you'll see around Penang, and these started their popularilty in the 1950s and 60s; vendors create compact balls of shaved ice and drench them in syrup. *Ice kacang* has evolved into extravagant combinations reflected in its other name, 'ABC', for *air batu campur* or 'mixed ice'. Ice cream, blobs of durian, chopped mango, banana, sapodilla, crushed peanuts or fruit jelly might be used, depending on what's in season and where you go. Palm seeds, called *attap chee*, are generally standard. Back in the day, the ice was shaved by hand-cranked machines but now motorised gizmos do the job very effectively. You order, and instantly an imposing icy mound appears in a bowl. Toppings and drizzles are deftly applied and the whole thing starts melting at once, before your eyes. ▷

CENDOL FROM PENANG ROAD FAMOUS TEOCHEW CHENDUL

Ice kacang at Prangin Mall

Kek Seng's famous ice kacang

Penang Road Famous Teochew Chendul

ICE KACANG

The point of this dish is that it's cooling; it's also texturally compelling. Chewy bits of agar-agar, creamy wads of canned corn, mushy sweetened red beans, soothing ice-cream, slushy, milk-soaked ice, dribbles of syrup, crunchy peanuts, and the slurpy, melted-together spoonfuls of mess that accumulate together in the base of the bowl make for one of the best antidotes to blistering tropical heat ever. And it's jubilant too, with its mad colours and oozing swirls of crazy, vegetal-fruity bits and pieces. Aficionados claim the ice must be cleanly shaven so it's light, flaky and melts in the mouth – it shouldn't be lumpy or crunchy.

Kedai Kopi Dan *ice kacang*

It's impossible to separate *ice kacang* from *cendol* (also spelled cendul or chendul). The two dishes are often sold together and are built on the same principle of shaved ice and syrup. *Cendol* (said as 'chen-dol'), it's thought, originated in Indonesia, and versions of it are common in Singapore and through Malaysia. Its name means 'swollen' and probably comes from the green, noodle-like rice flour 'worms' that make the dish so distinctive; their colour comes from pandan juice. (Luminous green versions will suggest food colouring.) Along with the shaved ice and 'worms', there's soft red beans, plenty of rich coconut milk and lashings of gooey palm sugar syrup. ✤

Cendol

Swatow Lane Ice Kachang

WHERE TO EAT

KEK SENG COFFEE SHOP
382-384 Jalan Penang,
George Town
8.30am-5.30pm, daily
The *ice kacang* here is incredibly famous – they make cute little agar-agar jellies to go on top and you can chose their homemade durian ice-cream (see pg 115) as an optional topping too. If you're a tourist, the staff have an almost clairvoyant sense of what you're here for. Before you know it, they'll have asked the kitchen for *'ais kacang taroh durian ais krim'* before you've even opened your mouth. This place has been operating since 1903 and oozes quaint, heritage ambience, so soak that up too.

SWATOW LANE ICE KACANG
102-E-1, New World Park, 102 Jalan Burma, George Town
9am-10pm, daily
In business since 1923, they've relocated from their original site to the airy New World Park Food Court (see pg 61), and the fourth generation of the Lee family now run the show. Combinations of fresh chopped fruits like papaya, banana and mango and a scoop of peanut ice-cream are their signature *ice kacang* flourishes. The fruit juices here are damned good too.

PENANG ROAD FAMOUS TEOCHEW CHENDUL
Lebuh Keng Kwee (at Penang Road),
George Town
10-30am-7pm, Monday-Friday, 10am-7.30pm, Saturday-Sunday
The queues are insane and when they're busy, the team behind this laneway cart throw *cendol* together like nothing you've ever seen – it's a frenzy of green 'worms', red beans, syrup, coconut milk and ice literally flying. You come because it's famous (around since 1936) and to say that you have, but the outlet at the nearby Prangin Mall (Ground Floor, 33 Jalan Dr Lim Chwee Leong, open 11am-9pm, daily) is a more chilled experience. Here you can order your *cendol* with a dumping of durian or *cempedak* – a distinctively flavoured jackfruit – when in season. They do an excellent, and generously sized, *ice kacang* as well.

KEDAI KOPI DAN ICE KACANG
84 Lorong Selamat, George Town
11am-5pm, daily
There are so many things to love about this small hawker centre patronised by locals. There's great *lor bak*, *rojak* and *char koay teow* and a spectacular syrup-drenched, ice-cream topped *ice kacang* that gets a big thumbs up from devotees.

ABC ICE KACANG,
Lebuh Presgrave, George Town
6pm-12am, daily
As evening falls, ABC, among the Presgrave hawker stalls, beckons. Finely shaved ice, plenty of creamed corn, a topping of peanut butter ice-cream and big, fat, unbroken red beans make for one impressive serve of *ice kacang*.

NYONYA DELIGHTS CAFE
191-193 Lebuh Victoria, George Town
10am-7pm (closed Monday)
In the touristy part of town and sandwiched between heritage buildings, this cosy, friendly place is famous for its homemade buns stuffed with chicken curry. But they do a mean *cendol* and *ice kacang* too. Sit at a front porch table and watch the street-life amble by (and your dessert melt in the warm air); it's a pleasant way to kill time.

LOKE THYE KEE
2 Jalan Burma, George Town
8.30am-9pm, daily
Their *ice kacang* and *cendol* have slurp, crunch, chew, chill and sweetness in all the right places and the staff are charming. They run a menu of local favourites which are nicely executed; the place should be busier than it sometimes is. It's an old, old business in a beautiful, renovated 1929 building.

A SELECTION OF *KUIH*
FROM A GEORGE TOWN
STREET VENDOR

Pronounced 'koi', like the goldfish, *kuih* (also '*kuey*' and '*koay*') means 'cake'. Dainty and jewel-like, these are bite-sized morsels like no other; they'll kick-start your morning, pick you up after lunch and propel you through the evening. So don't go quitting sugar just yet; Penangites sure as heck aren't.

KUIH

From the Nyonya cooking tradition (see pg 100), not all *kuih* are sweet. *Or kuih*, for example, is a steamed yam cake topped with dried prawns and green onion and *chai kuih* is a fat, steamed dumpling stuffed with shreds of carrot, yam bean and bits of dried prawn. Technically, curry puffs (or *kari pap*) and *pie tee,* a thin, crisp pastry shell with a sweet and spicy vegetable-based filling, are also classed as *kuih.* There are blue *kuih,* bright green ones, *kuih* striped pink and white, banana leaf-wrapped *kuih* and *kuih* rolled in coconut. Some are cut into neat squares or diamond shapes; others are slim cones or triangular dumplings, bound in banana leaves and steamed. Some of their colours come from natural sources such as pandan juice (bright green) and the blue pea flower (indigo blue, see pg 128). Main ingredients include sticky rice, rice, mung bean and tapioca flours, coconut milk, sago pearls and palm sugar. ▷

KUIH

The best *kuih* are handmade, which is time consuming. Traditionally, all the flours were freshly ground, coconut was freshly grated and the various colours carefully extracted from leaves, herbs and flowers. Making *kaya* (a jam used to top certain *kuih*) from scratch, using coconut, egg and palm sugar, involves hours of vigilant stirring over low heat. Textures of the finished *kuih* depend on proper preparations and cooking at the exact correct temperature for each item. Constant monitoring is necessary and some *kuih* rely on processes that evolve over two or three days. While most are cooked by steaming, other techniques include baking and frying. ❖

Pulut tai tai

Making 'turtle cake'

Blue Pea Flower

That beguiling blue colour you see in your *kuih* – and sometimes, your *nasi lemak* rice? It's from a small flower called *Clitoria ternatea*, butterfly pea or *bunga telang*. As per the Latin name, it does resemble Down South. Native to Indonesia and Malaysia, the flowers are high in antioxidants and have been used in traditional medicine to treat depression, anxiety, memory loss, asthma and epilepsy. But, back to that colour. It's extracted by sun-drying the flowers then soaking them in water; the flowers are strained out and the now-blue water is used for cooking. It's said to have a subtle floral flavour which gets kind of lost in the cooking process. Really, it's all about eating blue food.

Some types of Kuih

kuih bengka: a sweet, baked rice flour cake served in slices; it can be purple, green or brown. The tapioca version of this is called *kuih bengka-ubi*. Baked in banana-leaf lined trays, these were traditionally cooked using charcoal, imparting a slightly smoky edge.

kuih lapis: made by steaming thin, alternating layers of different coloured rice flour and coconut milk batter in a large tin. These are cut into diamonds to serve.

kuih talam: a two-layered cake, the top is made of coconut milk and rice flour; the bottom layer is made from mung bean flour and pandan leaf.

seri muka: similar to *kuih talam* but the top layer is a green pandan custard and the base is made of glutinous rice with coconut milk.

kuih dedar: delicious little pandan-scented pancakes rolled around a palm sugar-infused grated coconut filling.

pulut tai tai: glutinous rice compressed and cut into neat diamonds; coloured blue with pea flower and topped with blobs of *kaya*.

chai tau kuih: steamed, white radish cakes sprinkled with ground roasted peanuts.

pulut inti: glutinous rice, coloured with pea flower, topped with palm sugar and fresh, shredded coconut. Wrapped in a banana leaf in a pyramid shape, then steamed.

abuk abuk: a steamed cone of banana leaf; inside is a mix of sago, grated coconut, pandan juice and palm sugar.

pulut tekan huat kuih: cute steamed rice flour cakes in various colours (pink, green, white), with characteristic puffed-up tops.

onde onde: small, poached dumplings made from a rice flour dough stained green with pandan juice, stuffed with palm sugar and coated in grated coconut.

kuih angku: 'turtle' cake. Sticky rice flour and sweet potato dough stuffed with sweetened cooked mung beans, shaped in special wooden moulds, then steamed. The traditional colour is red but you'll see other colours too.

WHERE TO EAT

You'll find *kuih* stalls in markets and on the street, with hit-and-miss hours. These two places are sure bets and you can sit too.

KUIH NYONYA MOH TENG PHEOW
Jalan Masjid, George Town
10am-5pm (closed Monday)
Just off Lebuh Chulia, this is THE destination for *kuih*; it's more than 80 years old. Locals grumble they cut their cakes smaller these days but because pieces are tiny, this means you can try more. It's also a working factory and you can see *kuih* being made in the traditional manner with no shortcuts. The cognoscenti proclaim flavours here are the best on the island.

TASTE OF INDULGENCE
17 Lebuh Keng Kwee, George Town
9.30am-5.30pm, daily
In a handy location near Penang Road Famous Laksa (see pg 47) and Penang Road Famous Teochew Chendul (see pg 125), you can graze well in this laneway. Although there's no cooking action, the *kuih* choice is huge and they're proud of their product. The enthusiastic owner Julian is a realtor from KL who prefers selling cakes to condominiums. Sit in the old shophouse, order a juice or coffee and get your sugar fix – do try the *onde onde*.

"A veritable frenzy of retail options" isn't what first springs to mind when contemplating George Town. But don't write the shopping off just yet. Dig deep and you *will* discover tasty, useful, foodie-gifty items – except you don't need to dig. We've done that for you. Thank us later.

ANTIQUE CERAMICS & WOVEN RUNNER

If you're an antiques fiend, the curio stores in George Town can cause FOMO anxiety with their sometimes erratic opening times. **Lean Giap (443 Lebuh Chulia, 10.30am-6pm, closed Sunday)** keeps regular hours and a trove's worth of collectables, such as these assorted old bowls and spoons. Ottokedai **(174 Lebuh Victoria, 10am-7pm, daily)**, however, is no antiques store, with its funky mix of souvenirs and schmick interior. Find items like this gorgeous hand-loomed runner, from regional Malaysia, coloured using natural dyes and finely detailed with beads.

COFFEE & MUGS

You've fallen in love with Penang white coffee, so it's a done deal you'll take some home. Pick up a pack of venerable brand Koon Kee's sachets while you're chocolate provisioning at **The Chocolate Boutique** (see pg 132). The next order of business? What to serve it in. **Areca Books** is the best book shop in town – find beautiful tomes on local subjects, as well as select souvenirs. Like these adorable George Town mugs.

15 Jalan Masjid Kapitan Keling
9am-6pm, daily

JOSS STICKS

Banish lingering cooking smells with these. They're handmade by **Mr Lee**, one of the last joss stick makers in Penang. Now elderly, he plies his trade just to keep the tradition alive, and happily chats to customers. Intended for temple worship, they're crafted from sandalwood powder and a paste from the terja tree. Unlike commercial ones which are based on sawdust, the smoke from these doesn't harm lungs.

1 Lorong Muda
8am-11am, Mon-Fri

BISCUITS

Baking cakes, biscuits and festive treats since 1956, **Oh Eng Huat Cake Shop** is a treasure. Yes, there are more central, and more swept up cake shops dotted about, but this one has a resolutely traditional feel. Everything is made by hand and you might catch them turning out batches of *miku*, a sweet bun associated with ancestor worship that's a startling pink colour. Pick up some packs of their *tau sar pneah* (mung bean) biscuits, to bring home.

**78 Jalan C. Y. Choy
9.30am-10.30pm, daily**

CHOCOLATE

Housed in a converted mansion, **The Chocolate Boutique** is the best kind of tourist trap. Unless, of course, you don't like chocolate in which case – who *are* you? With more than 60 varieties, all made from Malaysian cacao, it's a tough crowd that can't find something here. The collections include bars and boxes, with flavours such as tiramisu, green tea, the usual nuts (almond, hazelnut et al) and, yes, durian.

**22 Lebuh Leith
9am-6pm, daily**

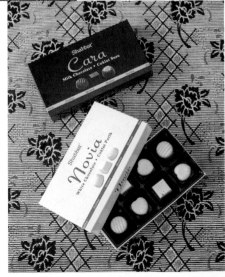

CAKE MOULDS

It's like a Malay Williams Sonoma; the keen home cook will be in heaven at retailer and wholesaler **Pots Kitchenware**. Packed with gadgets, woks, pots, ceramics, cleavers and so much more, there's stuff you won't easily find at home. Such as these adorable cake moulds, carved out of wood. The location is primo too; right in the thick of edible street things, near Chowrasta Bazaar.

**51 Jalan Kuala Kangsar
8am-5pm,
Monday-Saturday,
8am-12.30pm, Sunday**

PLACEMATS

Museum shops can be great sources of gifts and souvenirs and the one at the **Pinang Peranakan Mansion** is no exception. Once you've marvelled at the glorious displays and eclectic architecture, trawl the booty in the small store. Cards, porcelain, key rings, books and these lovely wooden placemats, in various colourways and emblazoned with double happiness and bat motifs, are typical.

**29 Lebuh Gereja
9.30am-5pm, daily**

DURIAN SWEETS

You're going to want to spend time cruising pretty Armenian Street, one of Penang's oldest, with its galleries and small museums, temples, knick knack shops and snack stops. Among the latter is **My Armenian Cafe** (see pg 119). Ever the durian freaks, they have a little shop next door where you can buy all manner of quality, packaged durian goodness; durian white coffee, freeze-dried durian, durian moon cakes and these cute lollies.

**98 Lebuh Armenian
10am-8pm, daily**

PEWTER CADDY

Pewter is an alloy of (mainly) tin, mixed with copper, bismuth and a few other metals. Malaysia is famous for it (it's the world's largest manufacturer) and, while Royal Selangor is the leading national brand, there are a few makers in Penang too. Scour the souvenir shops, such as **Hong Giap Hang**, for locally made pieces, like this handsome tea caddy. Highly durable, pewter requires little maintenance.

**308-312 Jalan Penang
7am-7pm
(closed Sunday)**

BELACAN

The throw-back nature of some George Town businesses is alluring. Take this gem, **Kwong Tuck Sundries & Liquors**, in a double-storey shophouse. The long counter, old-fashioned displays and friendly service speak of another retail era entirely. They're known for dried goods from Guangzhou and Chinese spirits, but it's a good place for some local *belacan* too. Lovely staff package it super well, to muffle that pong for travel.

**90 Lebuh Campbell
8am-5pm, daily**

SESAME OIL

Ghee Hiang is an old local brand, with several shops and a factory. It started in 1856 with a newly arrived Chinese pastry chef and grew from there. Today it's famous for traditional pastries as well as an iconic sesame oil; nothing tastes more sesame than this oil. Preservative and additive free, it comes either blended or 100% pure (red label). It's packaged in various sized bottles too, including travel-friendly 155ml ones.

**216 Jalan Macalister
9am-9pm, daily**

Notes

Penang In 12 Dishes
Published by RedPorkPress
P.O. Box 10003, Dominion Road, Auckland, 1446 New Zealand
www.redporkpress.com

 www.facebook.com/redporkpress
 www.instagram.com/redporkpress
 www.twitter.com/redporkpress

Publishing executive: Antony Suvalko
Editorial director: Leanne Kitchen
Art direction and design: Anne Barton
Copy editor: Judy Pascoe
Words and photography: ©RedPorkPress

©2018 RedPorkPress

First edition – April 2018

ISBN 9780473427290

Printed in China

PIG-SHAPED
RED BEAN CAKE
WITH TEA

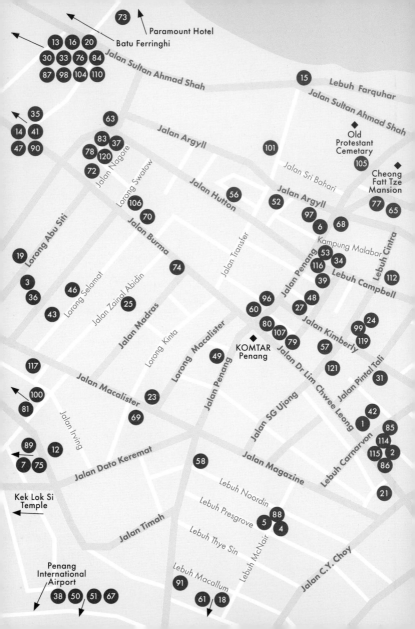